HAZLITT

and the Creative Imagination

WILLIAM HAZLITT
BY WILLIAM BEWICK
The National Portrait Gallery

HAZLITT

and the Creative Imagination

by W. P. Albrecht

THE UNIVERSITY OF KANSAS PRESS

LAWRENCE, 1965

Preface

WILLIAM HAZLITT'S COMPLETE WORKS, which fill twenty
closely printed volumes, include a great variety of materials colored by a variety of moods. However, despite
these infinite permutations of subject and object, the
basic ideas that Hazlitt developed as a young man remain a firm and dependable guide to understanding all
his work. Most useful in this respect is Hazlitt's concept
of the imagination. This has been discussed in various
specialized studies and most broadly—along with "the
development and expression of [Hazlitt's other] main
ideas"—in Herschel Baker's *William Hazlitt* (1962). I
am indebted to Professor Baker and to two other important studies that deal with Hazlitt's theory of the imagination: Elisabeth Schneider's *Hazlitt's Aesthetics* (1933)
and John W. Bullitt's article "Hazlitt on the Romantic
Conception of the Imagination" in the *Philological
Quarterly* for 1945. There have also been more recent
articles and unpublished dissertations on the subject.
Nevertheless, I think, the set of ideas covered by Hazlitt's
term *imagination* is important enough in Hazlitt's
thought, and in the Romantic period, to justify another
book.

The range of this book, obviously, is more restricted
than that of Professor Baker's, but on the subject of the
creative imagination it goes into more detail. I have not
attempted a biography of Hazlitt, the discovery of new
facts, or a critical study of even his more important
works; on the other hand, with respect to Hazlitt's writings and the works of predecessors and contemporaries,
my treatment is meant to be more comprehensive than

Professor Schneider's or Professor Bullitt's. Briefly, this book tries to analyze Hazlitt's theory of imagination; to trace its origins; to show, in the context of the controversy that followed Burke's *Reflections on the Revolution in France,* how the imagination is important in Hazlitt's political thought; to explain—in three of the seven chapters—Hazlitt's evaluation of literature from Shakespeare to Wordsworth according to its imaginative qualities; and finally to apply Hazlitt's criteria for imaginative writing to representative selections from his own works. Perhaps this approach runs the risk of isolating a more coherent pattern of ideas than the pluralistic Hazlitt always subscribed to; I have not, however, found any evidence to suggest that this pattern was not always basic in his thought.

As specified in the notes, chapters II, IV, V, and VI contain some materials from an earlier monograph of mine and from some of my articles. Permission to republish these materials is gratefully acknowledged. For reading and commenting on all or part of the manuscript, I am indebted to Professor Ralph M. Wardle of the University of Omaha, Professor Carl R. Woodring of Columbia University, and Professors Ethan P. Allen, Harold Orel, W. D. Paden, and Edward S. Robinson of the University of Kansas. I am also grateful to Professor Clyde K. Hyder, Editor of the University of Kansas Press, for his meticulous, scholarly, and understanding work on my MS; to the Yale University Library for permission to examine and quote from Hazlitt's autograph letters to Francis Jeffrey; to the University of Kansas for a research grant and for other arrangements that gave me some time to work on this project; to the staff of the University of Kansas Libraries; to my research assistant, Mr. Donald I. Yeats; and especially to my wife for typing, proofreading, and other kinds of help that would be difficult to describe. Without the generous assistance of others, there would have been many more errors than those still remaining, for which, of course, the responsibility is mine.

W. P. ALBRECHT

Lawrence
1 February 1965

Contents

Illustrations

I

Principles of Thought
and Action

> . . . the only pretension, of which I am tenacious,
> is that of being a metaphysician . . . —"On
> Envy" (1826).

As A STUDENT at the Unitarian New College in Hackney,
William Hazlitt read principally in what he called "the
material, or *modern* philosophy."[1] He learned a great
deal from the empirical philosophers—especially from
Hobbes, Locke, and Hartley—but he was repelled by
their mechanistic conception of the mind and by their
self-centered, necessitarian morality. His encounters
with the modern philosophy at Hackney led to his first
book, *An Essay on the Principles of Human Action*
(1805). The *Essay* marks the beginning of Hazlitt's life-
long insistence that the mind is creative, even in its simplest operations. Hobbes had modeled the mind after
the physical universe, and in explaining mental processes
in terms of physiological changes, he had—so Hazlitt
thought—reduced the mind to nothing but a machine
passively responding to sensory stimuli. A mind so conceived seemed to Hazlitt incapable of knowing or valuing. Hazlitt's interest was more than theoretical. As a
political writer he wanted to explain the psychology of
good citizenship; and as a critic he needed to analyze the
mental processes of the artist and the poet. He sought,

therefore, to revise Hobbes' model of the mind. Hazlitt retains the mind's dependence on the senses but stresses its ability to deal creatively with the materials of sensation. As Hazlitt describes it, the mind can mold these materials into ideas and symbols, to which, through sympathetic identification, it gives objective truth and moral urgency.

In the Renaissance truth had been regarded as an aspect of universal order knowable to the human mind. To gain insight into this universal order, man had to use his "reason." Reason had very broad powers. It was supposed to organize man's highest faculties into harmonious self-fulfillment, which both enlarged his understanding and freed his will from sensual appetite. Presented with sensory perceptions arranged by the imagination, it made use of logic, empirical wisdom, classical and Christian authorities, and supersensory insight to distinguish between truth and falsehood. In thus discerning the universal order, it directed the will toward realizing that order or, in other words, toward virtuous action.[2] In the age that produced Newton, however, the process of thought, the perception of values, and the causes of moral action all began to appear in a different light. In the *Leviathan* (1651) Hobbes restricted the source of all knowledge to sensory experience and defined thought as "motions of matter" set up by bodily contact with external objects.[3] He limited reason to logical thinking and reduced morality to self-centered prudence mechanically induced. Reason can infer certain "natural laws" according to which men may live peacefully together, but the underlying distinctions between good and evil are ultimately tested by "appetite or . . . aversion"—that is, by a subjective response rather than by an act of ratiocination dealing with objective reality.[4] In his *Essay Concerning Human Understanding* (1690) Locke fol-

EDMUND BURKE
BY SIR JOSHUA REYNOLDS
The National Portrait Gallery

JOHN LOCKE
BY SIR GODFREY KNELLER
The National Portrait Gallery

DAVID HARTLEY
BY JOHN SHACKLETON

lowed Hobbes in believing that all knowledge is derived from sensation and that good and evil are "nothing but pleasure or pain."[5] Locke's view of the mind is less mechanical than Hobbes'; but although he tried to make the "understanding" account for all mental activity, he had difficulty extending its processes, beyond the perception of empirical facts, to explain the recognition of stable moral values. Locke included revelation as a moral guide even when it goes *"against the probable conjectures of reason";* and, although he insisted on *"the eternal and unalterable nature of right and wrong,"* he took pains to show that in practice moral standards vary with the customs of different times and places.[6] Hartley, in *Observations on Man* (1749), denied that morality is "grounded on the eternal reasons and relations of things." He elaborated Hobbes' description of the mind as a mechanism and explained moral action as necessitated by previous associations with pleasure and pain.[7]

Taking issue with Hobbes, Locke, and Hartley, Hazlitt argued that the mind is autonomously creative rather than mechanically passive. He agreed with Hobbes that values are found in the way things affect a person and not in the things themselves, but he insisted that the idea of a "good" exists independently of one's self-interest, and that all the faculties of the mind must work harmoniously together to produce moral action. By Hazlitt's time the creative, value-perceiving, mind-integrating faculty had become the imagination. In the Renaissance the imagination was the faculty that received, compared, and combined sense impressions; whereas the reason was the ruling principle of the mind that ascertained the truth of these impressions and thus regulated the emotions leading to action. In the eighteenth century, as evident in Pope, Johnson, and Reynolds, reason had not altogether lost its place as the comprehensive faculty

dominating the other faculties of the mind; but after
Hobbes and Locke it had been increasingly thought of as
only the logical faculty—shorn of any mystical powers—
and as a guide to self-interested action rather than moral
truth. Francis Hutcheson recognized a "moral sense"
distinct from the understanding; and a similar isolation
of an aesthetic "sense" appears in Addison, Hutcheson,
and others. Identified by Addison as the aesthetic sense,
the imagination rose in the hierarchy of faculties to a position intermediate between the merely physical senses
and the moral one. It had its own moral powers—such as
providing aesthetic experience akin to religious feeling
—and it also gained prestige as the faculty that prompts
moral action through sympathetic identification with
others.[8]

The imagination finally assumed the role—once
played by reason—as the faculty which unifies the mind
in the process of apprehending truth and judging values.
Moreover, in order to define and communicate truth
and moral values, the imagination had to produce "new"
forms. The pre-Romantic poet could find his models
outside himself and structure them in a framework of
commonly accepted symbols, such as the God-Satan,
Heaven-Hell mythology of *Paradise Lost*. But in order
to evaluate the world of Hobbes and Locke, the Romantic poet was forced to create his own "truth" and "reality" by an act of the imagination and constrained to replace the old mythologies with symbols more appropriate to the world described by science. The Romantic
poet, therefore, faced the world in a uniquely personal
way. He could know truth or reality only in the act of
constructing it; and to give it communicable meaning,
he had to fuse thought, feeling, and sensation into generally moving symbols. Criticism acknowledged the imagination's creative role but also recognized that the com-

bining faculty could create a world too exclusively in the poet's own image. If the poet's symbols were to convey general truth to the general reader, the imagination needed to include some sort of control which would keep it from running off into subjective fantasy but which would still be sensitive to the immediate apprehension of truth. Coleridge found this sort of control in an "inward beholding" of truth, while Hazlitt depended on intuitive wisdom acquired through long experience.[9]

Whereas Coleridge steadied the imagination with supersensory knowledge, Hazlitt kept the control of the imagination within empirical limits. In itself, the idea of a world apprehended by the senses and put in order by the experienced mind was perfectly acceptable to him. His reading in speculative thought did not go far beyond the British empiricists and their French counterparts;[10] and if he disagreed with Hobbes, Locke, Hartley, and Helvétius on some points, he did not doubt that experience is the source of all ideas. Apparently he never thought of Coleridge's transcendentalism as anything but nonsense. For a time he looked hopefully to Kant "to explode [the] mechanical ignorance" of the empiricists, but he knew Kant only through commentators, who finally convinced him that Kant's system was a "wilful and monstrous absurdity."[11] To give validity to imaginative creation, he relied—not on supersensory disclosures—but on the solid "truth" of repeated experience. It is interesting to note that experience served Hazlitt's own imagination very well, for, unlike Coleridge, he wrote more imaginatively as he grew older.

Hazlitt's works fall into four groups, which—in roughly chronological order—are his philosophical writings, his political books and essays, his criticism of art and literature, and the essays of his last decade, which are loosely characterized as "familiar." Hazlitt's explanation of the mind and its operation is most detailed in his earliest work, where he protests, on the one hand, the restrictive psychology of the modern philosophers and, on the other, the tyranny of hereditary power. His political writings and what he calls his "metaphysics" are, in fact, correlative halves of his case for freedom. Whether dealing with psychological mechanism or with political tyranny, Hazlitt pins his hopes on the power of creative imagination to organize the whole mind and translate its synthesis of thought, feeling, and sensation into laudable moral operations. As Hazlitt turns to criticism, he finds the imagination no less important as the source of excellence in literature and art. Later, in his familiar essays, he continues to disparage any tendencies—inside or outside the mind—that would inhibit the sort of self-fulfillment that the creative imagination requires; and, especially in his later work, his own writing approaches his standards of imaginative excellence. Hazlitt was more concerned with writing for the present than the future; but if given his choice, he probably would have wished to be remembered as a metaphysician or as a defender of Napoleon and the French Revolution. Today, however, his philosophical and political writings are usually ranked below his criticism and the familiar essays which shape his old ideas, interests, resentments, and attachments into his own kind of art. If Hazlitt's treatment of his psychological theories is less thoroughgoing —and more interesting—in his later work, it is not because he has changed his mind about them or their importance, but because he has become a better writer whose imagination is more capable of assimilating and objectifying his ideas.

i

All his life Hazlitt wrote on "metaphysical" subjects,

but his two most substantial works on philosophy—the *Essay on the Principles of Human Action* and the *Lectures on English Philosophy*—come early in his career. They are perhaps his least attractive and certainly his most tedious books. But he set great store by them, especially the *Essay;* and although the prose lacks Hazlitt's later ease and vigor, there is no denying his earnestness as he expounds a set of ideas that always lay close to his heart. In 1793, at the age of fifteen, Hazlitt had entered the Unitarian New College in Hackney. Here he read the modern philosophers (although, he tells us, he did not read Hobbes until later), and began to shape his ideas for the *Essay*. In 1796, probably, Hazlitt left Hackney.[12] He returned briefly to live with his family in Wem, studied painting in Paris, had little success as a portrait painter, and in 1804 took up writing to make a living. Seven years after publishing his first book Hazlitt delivered his first series of lectures at the Russell Institution. Hazlitt's arguments against the "modern philosophy" survive, presumably, in the six essays printed for the first time in 1836, six years after his death, under the title *Lectures on English Philosophy*. Hazlitt touches on Berkeley, Hume, Hartley, Helvétius, Condillac, La Rochefoucauld, Mandeville, Bishop Butler, Horne Tooke, and others; but his principal targets are Hobbes and Locke.

A pamphlet called *Proposals for . . . A History of English Philosophy* (1809) is a good introduction to the *Lectures* and, in fact, immediately precedes them in Hazlitt's *Complete Works*. In this history, which was never written, Hazlitt planned to "lay the foundation of a system more conformable to reason and experience, and, in its practical results at least, approaching nearer to the common sense of mankind, than the one which has been generally received . . . within the last century."[13] By

"common sense" Hazlitt means the practical wisdom of
the nonspecialist, particularly as rendered intuitive by repeated experience. Hazlitt does not give the term the
special meanings that distinguish the Scottish "Common-
Sense School." The reality of external objects—which,
Thomas Reid had maintained, people commonly accept
along with the sensations caused by these objects—is
not a problem which concerns Hazlitt very much. Nor
does he allow common sense to affirm any intelligence
beyond man's own. Hazlitt's bent is always practical
and empirical. He has no use for the "incorporeal and
invisible forms of things." Bacon, by turning philosophy
away from such matters to a high regard for experience,
performed a great service; but in construing experience
as merely physical, Hazlitt adds, the modern philosophy
has "run from one error into another."[14] Hazlitt en-
larges the role of the mind: not only as free and creative
but as providing, in its own operations, an important
source of empirical data. Locke had "very fully and
clearly" established "that there are no innate ideas, . . .
if indeed so obvious a truth required any formal demonstration." But this is not to deny that the mind can
produce, modify, and arrange ideas. Locke failed to recognize that "our knowledge of mental phenomena," and
not external facts, is "the true basis of metaphysical enquiry." An examination of these phenomena will reveal
certain "innate principles of knowledge" (not "an innate knowledge of principles") according to which "our
ideas follow one another in a certain order." In the *Lectures* Hazlitt calls the whole complex of principles the
"faculty of reason," although elsewhere he defines reason
in different ways, usually as the abstracting, analyzing,
comparing, or calculating faculty. He uses the term *understanding* in a similar way, sometimes to mean the
mind itself—especially its active powers as distinguished

from sensation and memory—and sometimes to mean the merely logical or analytical faculty distinct from emotion and imagination.[15]

In the *Lectures* Hazlitt calls Hobbes "the father of the modern philosophy," but he admires Hobbes too much as a writer, and owes him too much as a philosopher, ever to take him to task as severely as he does the other modern philosophers. To Hazlitt's way of thinking, Hobbes had argued "reason" too far away from sensory experience; but Hazlitt finds that Hobbes' practice as a writer brought reason back down to reality. He cannot help admiring a man whose "strong mind and body appear to have resisted all impressions but those which were derived from the downright blows of matter: all his ideas seemed to lie like substances in his brain; what was not a solid, tangible, distinct palpable object was to him nothing."[16] Locke's style, on the other hand, strikes Hazlitt as redundant, cloudy, and ambiguous.[17] He is considerably harder on Locke, even though Locke had restored the mind to a more creative position than Hobbes would seem to allow. Hazlitt objects to Locke's metaphor of a blank sheet of paper because it suggests that the mind is "never acting, but always acted upon";[18] but Locke, of course, had gone beyond the limits of his metaphor. According to Locke, all ideas are either simple or complex. A simple idea is "not distinguishable into different ideas." Simple ideas may be perceived (1) by one sense only (blueness, sourness), (2) by more senses than one (extension, figure, rest, motion), (3) by reflection on operations of the mind about its other ideas (perception, volition, remembrance, faith), and (4) by both sensation and reflection (pleasure, pain). ". . . the mind is wholly passive in the reception of all its simple ideas"; but its complex ideas require some creative activity. The mind "exerts several acts of its own, whereby

out of its simple ideas" other ideas are framed: these are
(1) "complex ideas" made by combining "several simple
ideas into one compound one" (man, triangle), (2)
"ideas of relations" made by comparing two ideas (hus-
band, whiter), (3) and "general ideas" produced by abstraction.[19] Hazlitt, it turns out, departs from Locke
principally (1) in terminology, (2) in his emphasis on
the active role of the mind, and (3) in his refusal to accept a sharp distinction between particular and general
ideas. For Hazlitt all "ideas are the offspring of the understanding, not of the senses." Locke's simple ideas
"from one sense only" are not ideas at all, but only sensations, and none of Locke's other three kinds of simple
ideas can be attributed, as Locke had stated, to a "wholly
passive" mind. Every idea is the *product,* rather than
the *object,* of the understanding.[20] Even when he and
Locke agree—as they do, Hazlitt grants, regarding the
power of the mind to combine what Locke calls simple
ideas into complex ones—Hazlitt stresses the creative,
unifying power of the "superintending faculty" of the
understanding, which perceives the relation of sense impressions to one another by comparing and contrasting
them and fitting them intuitively into patterns established by previous experience. "Without this faculty, all
our ideas would be necessarily decomposed, and crum-
bled down into their original elements and fluxional
parts."[21] Hazlitt argues that the mind immediately
comes to grips with the phenomena of sensation and
shapes them into what he regards as, and simply terms,
"truth" or "reality."

In settling for this reality, Hazlitt is, in a sense, a bet-
ter-persuaded empiricist than Hobbes and Locke, on the
one hand, or Berkeley and Hume on the other. He rejects both the nominalism of the former and the skepticism of the latter. In his lectures "On Abstract Ideas"

and "On Tooke's 'Diversions of Purley,' " Hazlitt takes
up Hobbes' proposition that general ideas are only
names and Locke's "that they exist no where but in the
mind which perceives them."[22] All thoughts, says
Hobbes, originate in "SENSE," which is caused by some
"external body, or object" pressing on "the organ proper
to each sense." The sum of sensations is not, however, to
be mistaken for the external body; "the object is one
thing, the image or fancy is another." The retention of
"an image of the thing" after the "object is removed, or
the eye shut," is called *"imagination";* it is "but decaying sense," a farther step from the object itself. Words
are still another remove from actual objects. Compared
with "absolute knowledge" provided by sense and memory, words offer only *"conditional"* knowledge depending on exactness of definition. Words may be "singular
to one only thing" or "common to many things." In the
latter case they are called universals, "there being nothing in the world universal but names." Reason, which
deals with propositions containing general names, can
provide conclusions "not about the nature of things,
but [only] about the names of things."[23] In the *Lectures*
Hazlitt conceives of what he calls reason or understanding a good deal more broadly than this. He wants to
bring the reasoning process much closer to the phenomena of sense and their reality. Locke, too, had respect for
the particular—in fact, like Hobbes, he gave particular
ideas a clarity and validity lacking in generals; but he
did so, Hazlitt claims, at the expense of the mind. ". . .
all things that exist," says Locke, "are only particulars.
. . . When . . . we quit particulars, the generals that rest
are only creatures of our own making. . . ."[24] Hazlitt believes that *all* ideas are "creatures of our own making"
but none the less real or true on that account. He rejects Locke's firm distinction between the operations of

the mind that produce particulars and those that produce generals, and holds that, as it ascends through the
levels of abstraction, the mind continues to operate uniformly and creatively.[25]

As applied to ideas, Hazlitt points out, the terms *abstract* and *particular* are only relative.[26] The mind's
comprehension is necessarily so limited that it cannot
perceive the total number of parts and motions in any
object; therefore, in relation to the thing perceived, any
idea is necessarily abstract. "... in a strict sense all ideas
whatever are mere abstractions. . . ."[27] Hobbes and
Locke, of course, define abstract ideas in relation to particular ideas and not in relation to the external thing
that ideas are supposed to represent. Hazlitt, therefore,
has to face up to the "hard question" whether "our ideas
of things, however abstract and general, with respect to
the object they present, are not in their own nature, and
absolute existence particular." Every idea, he grants, is
sufficiently distinguishable from other ideas "for the actual purposes of thought"; that is, "the abstract idea of
a man" is not confused with "the abstract idea of a
horse or [with] the particular one of any given individual
man." But although ideas can be distinguished from
each other, no idea can be fixed within precise limits.
The various parts which an idea comprises are too varied, ambiguous, and unstable to add up to "absolute
unity." "Particular" ideas lack this precision even more
than the "confused and general" ones. The more "individual" an idea is, the less the mind can reconcile all the
complexities of time and space that it comprises, and the
more the integrity of the idea will suffer from an abundance of shifting sense impressions. As one tries to count
a rapidly moving flock of sheep, for instance, "his idea of
a particular number slide[s] into the general idea of
multitude."[28] What Hazlitt refuses to do, of course, is to

stay on any one level of abstraction; since he is more interested in the actual, dynamic process of thought than
in theoretical, static distinctions, he continually moves
from one level to another. He manages to ignore Rousseau's distinction: "Every general idea is purely intellectual; if the imagination meddles with it even a little,
the idea immediately becomes particular."[29] Hazlitt lets
his imagination meddle a good deal. In objecting also to
Berkeley's belief that there are only particular ideas,
Hazlitt points out that "without the general idea of a
line or a triangle, there could be no particular one . . ."
and, conversely, that even though the language of a geo-
metrical proof remains on one level of generalization,
one can follow it only by visualizing more specific geo-
metrical figures.[30] It would begin to look as though the
mind, for all its creativity, can't win. General ideas are
"confused," but particular ones "involve contradictions."[31] The difficulty is that truth or reality, as Hazlitt
sees it, cannot be confined to any of Hobbes' and Locke's
levels of abstraction or expressed in their literal denotative language. In Hazlitt's common-sense view, reality
is never a static thing. To find a faculty that can give integrity to this dynamic interplay between the general
and the particular, and provide a language to express it,
Hazlitt had to turn to the *imagination,* a faculty which
he considered much more comprehensive and creative
than the one which Hobbes called by the same name.
Hazlitt's appeals to experience with triangles and sheep
do not, of course, destroy Hobbes' and Locke's distinction between general ideas and particular ideas of substances (in fact, Hazlitt recognizes this distinction and its
practical value);[32] but they do point toward Hazlitt's
concern for the kind of truth that resides in neither the
particular nor the general but in a fluid combination of
both.

To show that the qualities of an object exist only in
the mind and not in the objects themselves, Berkeley and
Hume had presented an argument similar to Hazlitt's
case for the relativity of abstract ideas.[33] But for Hazlitt
their argument that the same object strikes the senses in
different ways under different conditions is "no argument at all" that the qualities of matter have no external
existence. Hazlitt makes the common-sense reply that if
"an object at a distance . . . does not look like the same
object near," this "is in consequence of the interposition
of the air, which gives it a different hue. . . ." The only
inference is "that one object has not the same sensible
qualities as another, or . . . that we do not know what the
true or natural qualities of each object are." Matter remains, for Hazlitt, "the cause of our sensations" and consequently the source of our ideas.[34] The investigation of
matter—its "difficulties and contradictions"—is nothing
that Hazlitt cares about. He is content with the sensations that matter provides for the general experience of
mankind—sensations from which the mind creates ideas
adequate to the problems of everyday living and with
which the imagination fuses thought and feeling to create a kind of truth excluded from the mutually exclusive
categories of Hobbes or Locke.

ii

It was only after literary criticism had become one of
his chief concerns that Hazlitt developed a full explanation of the imaginative process. Nevertheless the creative power of imagination to fuse sensation with thought
and feeling, and thus create an idea lively enough to im-
pel voluntary action, is central in his earlier work on
morals and politics. The *Essay on the Principles of
Human Action,* published seven years before Hazlitt delivered his *Lectures,* attacks the self-indulgent and me-

chanical morality of the modern philosophy. Here Hazlitt's principal opponents are Hobbes and Hartley. Within a commonwealth, Hobbes bases morality on individual self-seeking, with "reason" as the guiding faculty. Since reason is only "reckoning the consquences of general names" and since names are only more-or-less accurate designations of previous experiences remaining in the mind as images, reason is limited to apprehending efficient causes and their effects. Men may conceive that there is a final cause and call this cause God, but they cannot "have an idea, or image of him in [their] mind[s]" and therefore cannot *reason* concerning him. What a man can reason about in this limited world of sense, is the likely effect of certain causes on his continued and pleasant existence. Even without language—and therefore without reason—a man or an animal becomes more prudent as his experience furnishes him with multiple analogies to the present situation. Language enables man to extend this process by reducing his experience to "general rules," which can be combined in syllogisms to produce a demonstration.[35] From these general rules, the citizen of a commonwealth concludes that, if he is to safeguard himself and the fruits of his labor, he must "be contented with so much liberty against other men, as he would allow other men against himself" and, furthermore, that in order to restrain the liberty of all men at this point he must "confer all [his] power and strength upon one man, or assembly of men." Hobbes makes morality a matter of respecting, and government of safeguarding, the "means of peaceable, sociable, and comfortable living." Justice, gratitude, complaisance, facility to pardon, forbearance, respect, modesty, equity, and other virtues that make for peace among men are sanctioned by the basic right of self-preservation, and may be "contracted into one easy sum;

. . . that is, 'Do not that to another, which thou wouldest not have done to thyself.' "[36] Locke disagreed with Hobbes on some important matters—rejecting, for instance, Hobbes' proposition that a people do not have a right to dissolve their government—but in some passages he, too, strips the basic right down to self-preservation and from this premise deduces the rules of moral duty and political justice.[37]

According to Hobbes, and Hartley as well, moral actions—like all voluntary actions—are "necessitated." Voluntary actions, says Hobbes, "proceed from liberty"—that is, from the lack of any impediment—yet they also "proceed from necessity" because "every act of man's will, and every desire, and inclination proceedeth from some cause, in a continual chain, whose first link is in the hand of God the first of all causes."[38] Free will, says Hartley in his *Observations on Man* (1749), can be granted only if it is defined "in the popular and practical sense" as "the power of doing what a person desires or wills to do, of deliberating, suspending, choosing, &c. or of reshifting [various] motives."[39] In the chain of causes leading to voluntary action both Hobbes and Hartley assign great importance to association, especially with pleasure and pain. Images, says Hobbes, are linked in the memory by the circumstances of their original occurrence, and it is through their recurrence, thus linked in "trains of imaginations," that men and animals make—and act on—the causal connections that promise pleasure rather than displeasure.[40] Hartley goes further than Hobbes in detailing the mechanics of voluntary action. The association of pain or pleasure with certain experiences acts mechanically, through a system of vibrations, to produce all actions. External objects impressed upon the senses set up vibrations first in the nerves and then in the "white medullary substance of the brain." These vibrations are the cause of all our sensations, ideas, and motions. Sensations are distinguished from each other not only by the line of direction in which the vibrations enter the brain but by the region of the brain which is principally affected. When a sensation (A) is often repeated, it leaves a vestige or image of itself (a) which is called "a simple idea of sensation"; for the part of the brain so affected retains, for a time depending on the strength or frequency of the impression, "diminutive vibrations [or vibratiuncles] of the same kind" and, for a longer time, a disposition to respond to those vibrations peculiar to that idea.[41] If two sensations, A and B, repeatedly occur either simultaneously or consecutively, their vibrations will mutually modify each other, so that when A occurs alone and its vibrations are diffused throughout the brain, responding vibrations will occur not only in that part of the brain which responds to A but in that part where the vibratiuncles of B are situated. That is, A will "raise" b, which is the image or vestige of B. Similarly, association may link more elaborate sequences of images, so that the recurrence of one will activate all or some of the others. For instance, A having been associated with B, B with C, and C with D, the recurrence of A will stir up b, c, and d in that order. Or A, which was originally associated with C through B, may immediately activate c without the intervention of a less firmly impressed b. A number of simple ideas of sensation may be permanently consolidated into a "complex idea," for the simultaneous or consecutive recurrence of several impressions leaves a set of vestiges that will respond *in toto* to one of the impressions when it occurs singly. The smell of an apple, for instance, arouses and further cements the complex idea of the whole fruit. "It appears also from observation," Hartley adds, "that many of our intellectual ideas, such as those

that belong to the heads of beauty, honour, moral qualities, &c. are, in fact, thus composed of parts, which, by
degrees, coalesce into one complex idea."[42]

Hartley also uses the theory of vibrations to explain
muscular activity. He distinguishes "two sorts of motion, viz. automatic and voluntary, [of which] the first
depends upon sensation, the last upon ideas." A sensation or an idea comprises vibrations in the brain which
then pass into "motory nerves" to cause contraction of
the muscles.[43] Therefore, association can establish similar vibratory patterns among sensations, ideas, and
motions, so that the occurrence of one part of such a
complex will set the whole thing off. A motion may result "automatically" from some sensation (as one recoils
from a hot stove); "voluntarily" from "that idea, or state
of mind (i.e., set of compound vibratiuncles), which we
term the will"; or "semi voluntarily" from some idea,
sensation, or motion that has become associated with an
action that was originally voluntary (upon hearing his
train whistle, for instance, a commuter may "semi voluntarily" break into a run).[44] In every case the motion is
determined by vibrations, which are either the immediate effect of certain impressions, or the remote
compound effect of former impressions, or both. An essential link in the chain of cause and effect that leads to
voluntary action is some previous association with pain
or pleasure. This is true of both selfish and disinterested
action. If we act for the benefit of another, it is because
in the past we have associated his welfare with our own
pleasure, and the set of vibrations which we call the will
is put in action by the memory of that pleasure and carried over into muscular activity. Children are at first
completely selfish in their desires, but through the association of their own pleasure with the happiness of their
parents, for instance, they come to desire their parents'

happiness as much as their own.[45] Thus, Hartley concludes, the moral sense of judgment is not "an instinct" or something "grounded on the eternal reasons and relations of things" but simply the necessary product of association with one's own pain or pleasure.[46]

The *Essay on the Principles of Human Action* answers Hobbes and Hartley by rejecting (1) the apparent exclusion of mental activity from voluntary behavior and (2) the translation of morality into basic selfishness. To support these rejections, Hazlitt relies on the power of the imagination to create ideas by fusing the general and the particular and to establish sympathy with others. He categorically denies Hartley's doctrine of vibrations as unfounded and unproved, confessing, however, that he stands "merely on the defensive"—with "no positive inferences to make" but only "a common-sense feeling against the refinements of a false philosophy." If Hartley's theory were true, a vibratory motion would excite *all* the ideas stored in the brain. Hartley's explanation is "like supposing that you might tread on a nest of adders twined together, and provoke only one of them to sting you."[47] For his own theory of the imagination, Hazlitt owes a good deal to Hartley's associationism (without the vibrations), but he argues that associationism alone cannot account for voluntary actions, because the situation in which we act never corresponds exactly with a previous pattern of association. If a child avoids running into some kind of object he has never seen before, it is because "he takes the old idea of pain which subsisted in his memory, and connects it by that act of mind which we call imagination with an entirely *new* object."[48] Although, in explaining voluntary action, Hazlitt must think of imagination as dealing with "what has merely an imaginary [or future] existence," he would avoid "associating the word *imagination* with merely fictitious situations and events, that is, such as never will have a real existence." Imagination creates a *"real interest"* in the future event by presenting it concretely, and not as "a merely abstract idea."[49] When a child seeks or avoids an object, the object is associated with something in the child's memory, and the child's selection among various courses of action is limited by his previous experience; but within these conditions the imagination must still *create* a lively idea of good or bad and the understanding (the faculty that relates cause and effect) must determine the means of attainment or prevention. Therefore, Hazlitt concludes, the imagined good's "tendency to produce action is not entirely owing to the association between the original impression, and a particular action, which it mechanically excites over again."[50]

With this latter statement Hartley would have had to agree; for, despite his emphasis on the role of association as ultimately determining all motives, he does not exclude abstraction, comparison, or rational selection from the activities of the mind that lead to voluntary action.[51] Nor does Hobbes, who believes that voluntary action follows a comparison of alternative courses and an ultimate selection among them according to the promise of *"praise, dispraise, reward,* and *punishment."*[52] Hazlitt gladly acknowledges that Hobbes, by assigning an important role to such causes, "properly defines a moral agent to be one that acts from deliberation, choice, or will."[53] In fact, Hazlitt gives his "full and entire assent" to the doctrine of necessity demonstrated "over and over again . . . by Hobbes, Hume, Hartley, Edwards, Priestley, and others." For Hobbes has shown "that necessity is perfectly consistent with human liberty" and "moral reasoning."[54] Nevertheless Hazlitt feared that unwarranted inferences from Hobbes' statements of his doctrine of necessity would destroy "the ground-work of morality"

by suggesting that the mind is the helpless victim of
"blind impulse" and unresponsive to the "excitement of
reason."[55] For instance, Hobbes uses the word *freedom*
in two different senses when he says that a man "hath
freedom to do if he will" (that is, the action resulting
immediately from his willing it is not impeded) but that
he lacks "freedom to will" (that is, his will and its "ad-
hering" action are the only possible result of the causes
leading up to them).[56] Hazlitt sees no reason why the
word *free* (meaning lack of impediment but not freedom from causation) should not be applied to both
operations: "The body is said to be free when it has the
power to obey the direction of the will: so the will may
be said to be free when it has the power to obey the dic-
tates of the understanding."[57]

iii

Free within the channels of necessity to respond to
the powerful reality of the imagination and to follow
the foresighted counsels of the understanding, the will is
not bound to a mechanical self-indulgence. The design
of the *Essay on the Principles of Human Action* is "to
shew that the human mind is naturally disinterested, or
that it is naturally interested in the welfare of others in
the same way and from the same direct motives, by
which we are impelled to the pursuit of our own interest." By "natural disinterestedness" Hazlitt does not
mean a set of innate moral ideas or, like Shaftesbury and
Hutcheson, an innate moral sense which responds pleas-
urably to the moral alternative, but, rather, one of those
"innate principles" which Hazlitt discovered in the operation of the mind. This principle is a "natural" attraction to happiness which is not necessarily either self-
centered or benevolent but which may be turned in either direction by habit and custom. Voluntary actions,

unlike involuntary ones, do not arise solely from one's desire to avoid what is painful to himself or to gratify his own desires, but may be determined by the "idea" of good independent of one's own pleasure or pain. ". . . the mind is naturally interested in it's own welfare in a peculiar mechanical manner, only as far as relates to it's past, or present impressions"; for, since the sensations that a person will experience in the future cannot react mechanically upon his present self, only the imagination can connect his present self with his future self, and therefore it alone can produce ideas to motivate voluntary action. In other words, memory and sensation limit "personal identity" to the past and the present; it is only as far as these two faculties are concerned that man is "a personal, or if you will, a selfish being."[58]

Since a mechanical sympathy with one's future sensations does not exist, there must be "something in the very idea of good, or evil, which naturally excites desire or aversion," and there must be, consequently, the same psychological basis for interested and disinterested action. Hazlitt, unlike Hartley, does try to ground morality "in the eternal reasons and relations of things." ". . . the desire for happiness is natural to the mind . . . in the same manner that it is natural to the eye to see when the object is presented to it. . . ."[59] We seek the good of another person not because, as Adam Smith seems to say, we share his suffering and therefore act automatically to reduce his pain and our own, but because the removal or avoidance of another's pain is a good in itself and immediately recognized as such. The power of exciting desire "inheres in the very nature of the object."[60] Hazlitt, of course, cannot be saying that values lie in objects themselves rather than in their effects on sentient beings or that this effect does not depend on association. But he is arguing that how much one values a certain good depends ultimately on its "distinctness" and not on the person it benefits. If a person favors his own happiness or that of a friend, it is because ignorance or habit has made the happiness of others less vivid to his imagination and therefore less compelling.[61] ". . . a sentiment of general benevolence can only arise from an habitual cultivation of the natural disposition of the mind to sympathise with the feelings of others by constantly taking an interest in those which we know, and imagining others that we do not know, [whereas artificial] self-interest . . . must be caused by a long narrowing of the mind to our own particular feelings and interests, and a voluntary insensibility to every thing which does not immediately concern ourselves."[62]

Hartley, too, assigns imagination an indispensable role in moral action; but he gives imagination a lower rank among the activities of the mind than Hazlitt does and a much less comprehensive function. Memory, he says, recalls sensations and ideas in about the "same order and proportion" as they originally occurred; whereas "imagination or fancy" selects and combines ideas— "especially visible and audible ones, in a vivid manner" —according to established patterns of association but "without regard to the order of former actual impressions and perceptions."[63] Imagination involves a higher degree of intellectual activity than sensation or memory but does not offer pleasures that are permanently satisfying (as *The Prelude* and "Tintern Abbey" remind us). ". . . it is evident, that the pleasures of imagination were not intended for our primary pursuit, because they are, in general, the first of our intellectual pleasures, which are generated from the sensible ones by association, come to their height early in life, and decline in old age." Along with the pleasures of "sensation," "ambition," and "self-interest," the pleasures of the imagination are

principally derived from association with sensations or
with "simple ideas of sensation," whereas the pleasures
of "sympathy," "theopathy," and "the moral sense" are
associated with more complex and therefore more intellectual ideas. Imagination serves the moral sense, however, by providing "a relish for natural and artificial
beauty" which, by association, serves to "generate and
augment" the "social, moral, and religious affections."[64]
For Hartley, association coalesces the pleasures of imagination with those of the moral sense; and moral action
results when these pleasures activate the "set of compound vibratiuncles" that Hartley terms "the will." For
Hazlitt, however, the imagination has a more dominant
role. It not only supplies vivid images that enter into the
idea of a "good" but charges them with habitual thought
and feeling to "create" the sympathetic object of voluntary action. For Hartley, association makes use of the
imagination to whet the pleasures of morality; for Hazlitt, the imagination makes use of association to create an
idea of good which is "naturally" attractive without any
necessary reference to personal pleasure or pain.

In his "Remarks" on Helvétius published with the
Essay in 1805 and expanded in his *Lectures on English
Philosophy*, Hazlitt continues his case for natural disinterestedness. Hazlitt himself was too much of a modern
philosopher to oppose Helvétius' argument "that the
habitual or known connexion between our own welfare
and that of others, is one great source of our attachment
to them, [and] one bond of society," but he wants to
show that benevolence has "a natural basis of its own to
rest on."[65] Paraphrasing "Hobbes's maxim that 'pity is
only another name for self-love,'" Helvétius had written, "My sympathy with the sufferings of another is always in exact proportion to my fear of being exposed to
the same sufferings myself."[66] In the *Lectures* Hazlitt

quotes Bishop Butler, who in 1726 had rejected Hobbes' proposition with an appeal to experience and common sense that Hazlitt of course found very congenial. The existence and nature of good-will, Butler points out, is "a mere question of fact or natural history, not proveable immediately by reason." But historical facts and actions, the "testimony of mankind," and a scrutiny of our own "inward feelings upon sight of persons in distress" all support "some degree of benevolence amongst men" and, in addition to some selfish feelings, "real sorrow and concern for the misery of our fellow-creatures."[67] Examining his own feelings, Hazlitt decides that the strongest inclination is not always to avoid pain and that one often chooses benevolent action rather than pleasure, even when such a choice is a painful one. What benevolence aims at is not to remove "the idea or immediate feeling of pain from the individual" himself, but to disconnect the "idea of pain" from "the idea of another person." The connection between these two ideas is entirely different from that between a feeling of pain and a wound inflicted on one's own body; the latter connection is "an affair of sensation," the former "an affair of imagination."[68] Even if we should act benevolently only to relieve our own uneasiness, there would still be no merely mechanical operation of the will, for the imagination would still have to identify us with the person in distress. This kind of self-love, moreover, could not be called indifference to the good of others; and on the basis of its *effects, "disinterested benevolence"* could still be distinguished from "deliberate, calculating selfishness."[69]

Hazlitt's belief that morality is unselfish continues to have the validity of the common sense in which it is rooted, a kind of validity that modern psychology has come to recognize as basic to more systematic study, especially in "interpersonal relations." The conviction that morality is disinterested is part of the content of "common-sense or naive psychology" that cannot be contradicted by experiment. The goals of moral action are generally felt to have an attraction independent of expediency;[70] or, to put it Hazlitt's way, good is "naturally" attractive regardless of the person it seems to benefit. Hazlitt's understanding of free will also fits readily into the matrix of common-sense psychology and has maintained the same kind of validity.[71]

iv

Accurately assessing its style, Hazlitt called the *Essay* "that dry, tough, metaphysical *choke-pear*."[72] Nevertheless, in 1819, he ranked it highest among his works; he frequently repeated its arguments; and in 1828, two years before his death, he still thought it contained "an important metaphysical discovery, supported by a continuous and severe train of reasoning, nearly as subtle and original as anything in Hume or Berkeley."[73] Hazlitt's claim to originality is not groundless even though the *Essay* draws heavily on ideas that were current in the eighteenth century. Shaftesbury, Hutcheson, Reid, and others had described various intuitive moral senses; and moral intuition had frequently been connected with the imagination. Dugald Stewart had pointed out that "the apparent coldness and selfishness of mankind may be traced, in a great measure, to a want of attention and a want of imagination."[74] It is through the imagination, Adam Smith had explained, that we conceive "what other men feel," and it is only when our sympathies are thus awakened that we achieve the "amiable" virtue of helping others or the "respectable" virtue of restraining our own disagreeable passions out of respect for others' feelings. We respond to another's "pain or distress . . . in proportion to the vivacity or dulness" of our conception of his plight.[75] According to Hume, Lord Kames, and

Priestley, the power of imagination to stimulate moral action depends on the vividness of the imaginative conception, and this vividness diminishes with the remoteness of the subject, in time and space, from one's habitual concerns.[76] Hazlitt's originality does not lie in using the imagination to account for moral intuitions, but in keeping these intuitions independent of extra-rational support and, at the same time, in avoiding the mechanistic implications of Hobbes and Hartley. Although always staying within the empirical framework of the modern philosophy, Hazlitt refuses to reduce the mind to a machine. In all of its operations, Hazlitt insists, the mind is the creative master and not the mechanistic slave of sense impressions.

Hazlitt's "dicovery," however, is hardly enough to make the *Essay* a major contribution to speculative thought. The *Essay* and Hazlitt's supplementary writings on metaphysics are interesting today mainly because they re-assert the importance and freedom of the mind and because they synthesize into a theory of the imagination the powers which had been attributed to this faculty during a long period of re-evaluation. This theory, with a few added refinements, was to serve Hazlitt well during the rest of his life: in his political essays, his criticism, and his familiar essays. Hazlitt's definitions of the imagination are not entirely stable, but the *Essay* establishes certain qualities which are likely to characterize this faculty whenever Hazlitt discusses it and its achievements. As defined in the *Essay,* the imagination is not, by any means, uninformed, undirected fantasy. It requires knowledge of the person sympathized with and of all the attendant circumstances, and it includes the ability to relate cause and effect and thus foresee "the probable or necessary consequences of things."[77] The sympathetic identification that leads to moral activity is therefore an act of "reasoning imagination." Hazlitt explains that he does not "use the word *imagination* as contradistinguished from or opposed to reason, or the faculty of which we reflect upon and compare our ideas, but as opposed to sensation or memory."[78] It is by "multiplying, varying, extending, combining, and comparing [one's] original passive impressions"—by thus "push[ing] his ideas beyond the bounds of his memory and senses"—that the imagination brings the predicted idea of good and evil alive in all its emotion-charged particulars and thus "*creates* the object" that incites voluntary action.[79] This process begins with "the feelings connected with [individual images]" and builds up an elaborate complex of ideas as these images are allowed to exert the full force of association under the impetus and selective control of feeling.[80] Clearly anticipated in the *Essay,* therefore, is the definition of imagination that is of basic importance to his political writings and to his criticism: a comprehensive faculty which, when conditioned by sympathetic identification and excited by emotion, brings all the powers of the mind harmoniously into play to produce moral action or to mold the phenomena of sensation into truth and reality.

II

Political Ideas

> I am no politician, and still less can I be said to be party-man; but I have a hatred of tyranny, and a contempt for its tools . . . —*Political Essays* (1819).

HAZLITT WAS NOT quite eleven when France revolted against the Bourbons, and he was only five when his family had sought freedom under another revolution. The Reverend William Hazlitt, the friend of Joseph Priestley and Richard Price and the acquaintance of Benjamin Franklin, had befriended American prisoners in Ireland and spoken openly for American independence. In 1783 he took his family to America, where they lived until William's ninth year. The Hazlitts returned to England in 1787, and six years later William entered the Unitarian New College at Hackney, which had been founded by a group of his father's friends, including Drs. Price and Priestley.[1] Religious dissent furnished the chief support for English radicalism, but the students at Hackney seem to have gained a special reputation for revolutionary zeal.[2] Hazlitt remained at Hackney from 1793 to probably 1796, years which defined for Hazlitt the political issues which were to concern him throughout his life.

In 1790 Burke's *Reflections on the Revolution in France* aroused the English people, and not merely the aristocracy, to a fear of the French nation and of a possi-

ble English revolution. In 1793 England declared war
on republican France and, less formally, upon civil liber-
ties at home. The years 1794 and 1795 were marked by
scarcity and unrest. Societies of working men were sup-
pressed, and their leaders prosecuted.[3] The apologists
for liberty were on the defensive, and the working
classes, without representation in Parliament and denied
the right to organize, faced two decades of recurrent hard
times. Thus it was in a place of liberal and revolutionary thought, and in a time when many Englishmen apparently feared liberty more than its loss, that Hazlitt
formulated not only his metaphysics but his political
ideas as well. Hazlitt tells us that he began "A Project
for a New Theory of Civil and Criminal Legislation"
(1836) in 1792 and, while at Hackney, submitted a draft
of it to his tutor "in lieu of the customary *themes*."[4]

The *Essay on the Principles of Human Action* and
the "Project" are alike in owing a great deal to the modern philosophy and, at the same time, in rejecting its mechanical and self-centered explanation of thought and
action. In defining the powers of government, Hazlitt
accepts the limited political world of Hobbes, even
though—like Hobbes himself—he recognizes that it is an
abstraction excluding important kinds of human experience. Men in a state of nature, Hobbes had said, are
equally free to pursue their selfish desires, but in order
to preserve this freedom and equality in competition
with others, they are impelled by self-love to exchange
a state of nature for a commonwealth.[5] The function of
government is (1) to define the point to which the individual may pursue his selfish desires while still allowing
others the same freedom and (2) to prevent aggressors,
domestic or foreign, from going beyond this point. Hazlitt agrees to all this, but he is not laying aside his usual
skepticism of selfish calculation as a guide to moral be-

havior. He puts his political world within the context of a moral world, with a causal connection between the two. The moral context in which a democratic society can come into being and survive is not one in which enlightened selfishness identifies the good of each with the good of all but a work of the imagination requiring of its citizens—individually and collectively—complete self-realization in thought, feeling, and action. This moral context is not the mechanical product of physical sensation and selfish calculation but, rather, the projection of an inner harmony achieved in freedom.

Good government and good art put similar demands on the imagination; and most of Hazlitt's political writings—like his essays on painting and literature—are directed against those forces that would inhibit the imagination and, therefore, lead to "abstraction" rather than individual completeness. Hazlitt's political ideas may be most clearly defined in relation to Burke's *Reflections on the Revolution in France,* not only because many of his political works are, directly or indirectly, replies to Burke but also because Burke and his opponents represent different causes of abstraction. Burke and Hazlitt are alike in accepting the imagination as a moral guide and in distrusting any political scheme based on a selfish calculation of consequences. For Hazlitt, however, a powerful aristocracy is not, as Burke insists, a repository of wisdom and virtue but an obstacle to free inquiry and therefore to the full development of individual citizens. Among Burke's opponents Mackintosh, Paine, and Godwin held views on practical politics much more acceptable to Hazlitt than Burke's; but since all three tried to justify natural rights by an appeal to enlightened self-interest and relied on reason to disclose an identity of interests, they represent another kind of abstraction that Hazlitt persistently opposes, in art as well as in politics.

Godwin is also important, in a discussion of Hazlitt's political ideas, because his *Political Justice* (1793) provoked Malthus' *Essay on Population* (1798), a work to which Hazlitt devotes a long book and many essays. Malthus, who applied utilitarian principles to political measures that Hazlitt found abhorrent, represents a further degree of narrowing—to dangerous selfishness and arid rationalism—which Hazlitt found characteristic of his age.

i

Speaking before the Revolution Society on 4 November 1789, Dr. Richard Price delivered the sermon that provoked the *Reflections on the Revolution in France*. The Revolution Society comprised mainly Dissenters but also some Anglican members of both Houses of Parliament. It had been formed to honor the 1688 Revolution, the principles of which, Dr. Price declared, the French people had successfully reasserted. The *Reflections* begins by attacking Dr. Price's sermon and goes on to expound the faults and dangers of revolutionary doctrines and to exhibit the atrocities already committed by the French revolutionary government. In this and other works, Burke rejects any implication in the 1688 Revolution that government exists only by the consent of the governed[6] or that natural rights persist in modern society. Burke distinguishes between an antecedent state of barbarous "nature" and the "natural" functions of government in civilized society. He admits that, prior to entering civil society, man possessed certain "natural rights"—self-defense, judging for himself, asserting his own cause, even, as Hobbes said, a "right to everything" —but this state is one of barbarism, of "our naked, shivering nature," before man had come to know virtue. "These metaphysic rights entering into common life, like the rays of light which pierce into a dense medium, are, by the laws of Nature, refracted from their straight line." Since government exists for the advantage of men, men have a right to the advantages that government can provide, but these advantages must always be ascertained in relation to the existing situation and not inferred from any abstract or prior distinction between good and evil. ". . . in proportion as [theoretical rights] are metaphysically true, they are morally and politically false." The advantages of government, in which the real rights of men consist, often lie "in balances between differences of good,—in compromises sometimes between good and evil, and sometimes between evil and evil."[7]

Despite this relativism of practical good and evil, Burke believes in a moral order sanctioned by divine intent, an order which it is the function of government to ascertain and enforce and with which the continued existence of a government signifies accord. Burke lays "the foundation of government . . . in a provision for our wants and in a conformity to our duties: it is to purvey for the one, it is to enforce the other." But these duties are not merely the reciprocals of the "imaginary rights of men."[8] Burke does not agree with Hobbes that government draws a circle within which men are completely free to do as they please and outside of which they must restrain themselves only out of respect for a compact designed to protect their own selfish interests. Men in society are never morally independent of each other and never have "the right . . . to act anywhere according to their pleasure, without any moral tie." Their wills must be continually curbed out of respect for "obligations to mankind at large, which are not in consequence of any special voluntary pact [but which] arise from the relation of man to man, and the relation of man to God."[9] It is the function of government to exercise this continual

restraint. Government should always oppose reason,
prudence, and virtue "to will and to caprice."[10] Among
men's "wants" (i.e., *needs* rather than desires) that government should provide for, Burke includes "the want
. . . of a sufficient restraint upon their passions."[11] The
"Parisian philosophers," Burke charges, "explode or render odious or contemptible, that class of virtues which
restrain the appetite," and substitute a permissive kind
of virtue called "humanity or benevolence."[12] It is this
sort of moral looseness, he says, that hardens the heart
and leads to such terrors as those of the Revolution.

Burke disagrees with Hobbes and Locke not only on
what virtue is but on how it is known and encouraged.
Using the same pejorative modifier that he applied to
man's "shivering nature," Burke argues that "naked reason" is insufficient for moral judgments or for constructing the truly natural order of society. It lacks "the
wardrobe of a moral imagination, which the heart owns
and the understanding ratifies." "Prejudice" and "prescription" are the strongholds of clothed, or genuine,
reason against the merely naked variety. Having previously engaged "the mind in a steady course of wisdom
and virtue," prejudice enables a man to act decisively
and firmly within the "uniformly continued sense of
mankind."[13] The "first of our prejudices"—the church
—instills selflessness and hope of immortality "into persons of exalted situations" and "operate[s] with a wholesome awe upon free citizens."[14] Another prejudice is
aristocracy. "Bred in a place of estimation"; with leisure
"to read, to reflect, to converse"; "enabled to take a large
view of the wide-spread and infinitely diversified combination of men and affairs in a large society," the aristocracy provides a continuity of virtue and wisdom to guide
and protect "the weaker, the less knowing, and the less
provided with the goods of fortune." By fostering this

aristocracy, civil society has cultivated man's reason—his virtuous wisdom rather than his naked calculation—and so evolved into a "state of Nature" which is "much more truly so than a savage and incoherent mode of life."[15] Prescription has also had a share in this evolutionary process. The term *prescription* is taken from the law of real property, and refers to a title based on ancient and unquestioned possession.[16] The English constitution is a prescriptive one "whose sole authority is, that it has existed time out of mind." It embodies the tested wisdom of "the species" as a bulwark against the momentary foolishness of either the individual or the multitude.[17] A "permanent body composed of transitory parts," it has attained "a just correspondence and symmetry with the order of the world."[18]

As determined by the kind of reason that is steadied by prejudice and prescription, the true rights of men are their "wants" or "advantages."[19] These rights include the right to live by law; "to justice; . . . to the fruits of their industry, and to the means of making their industry fruitful; . . . to the acquisitions of their parents, to the nourishment and improvement of their offspring, to instruction in life and to consolation in death."[20] One must note that this list excludes two rights that were basic in revolutionary thought and action: (1) the right of the governed to dissolve a government that has failed to secure their rights and (2) the people's right to be represented in government. In view of the Glorious Revolution, Burke cannot say that the people may never alter the established government; but he insists that except in cases of strictest necessity the people are bound by the compact they have entered into. Burke defends the Revolution of 1688, but only as "an act of *necessity,* in the strictest moral sense in which necessity can be taken."[21] Burke also opposed anything like majority

rule, even through elected representatives. His occasional statements that "the people are the natural control on authority" and that "in all forms of government
the people is the true legislator"[22] are not to be taken in
any strictly democratic sense. Burke sees neither "policy," "utility," nor "right" in considering a numerical
majority of all citizens as "the people" or their will as
law. The concept of "the people" is appropriate only to
civil society and is translated into actuality only under
the discipline that this artifact imposes. "The people"
are not necessarily *all* the people or even the majority.
What "constitutes the people, so as to make their act the
signification of the general will" is determined not by
their numbers but by the "specific conventions in each
corporation." In a society where reason is "cultivated
and most predominates," Burke recognizes "the PEO-
PLE" as "great multitudes act[ing] together, under that
discipline of Nature." This, however, is not a matter of
the majority determining the general will, but of "the
common sort of men" in harmonious subordination to
"their proper chieftains."[23] Elsewhere, Burke limits
"the people" to the chieftains. ". . . those who, in any
political view, are to be called the people" he defines as
"those of adult age, not declining in life, of tolerable
leisure for [political] discussions, and some means of in-
formation, . . . and who are above menial dependence
(or what is virtually such). . . ." The number of these in
England and Scotland Burke estimated at about 400,000
out of a population of over 10,000,000.[24] Three years
earlier, taking an even more exclusive view, he had numbered "the people of England" at less than 35,000.[25]
Burke grants that "actual" wisdom and virtue may exist
outside the class where it can be presumed, but "no rota-
tion; no appointment by lot; no mode of election" can
be counted on to discover it. Burke does not "hesitate

to say that the road to eminence and power, from obscure condition, ought not to be made too easy." Ability as well as property should be represented in government, but at the same time property, the indispensable factor in perpetuating society, must be protected.[26] Burke was not much concerned with spreading enlightenment by education or public discussion. The gift of criticism that Arnold praised in Burke[27] was not one that Burke encouraged among subordinates in the established order. Nor, as a means of fostering virtue and wisdom among the unlanded, did he look very far beyond the church and the restraints imposed by that other great stronghold of prejudice, the aristocracy—just as he was content, even in a time of scarcity, to leave the laborer's standard of living to the machinery of supply and demand.[28]

ii

Within three years the many replies to Burke's *Reflections* included books by Mackintosh, Paine, and Godwin, all of whom—in defending natural rights—bolster antecedent nature with the principle of utility. Whereas Burke had refused to stay within the rational framework of the *Leviathan,* these writers oppose him by trying to strengthen that framework. In the face of Burke's denunciation of any system based on reason alone, they try to make their case for natural rights more reasonable— by connecting these rights with general happiness. In *Vindiciae Gallicae* (1791) James Mackintosh speaks for the Whigs who supported Charles James Fox. He argues for the right of all citizens to share in the government, directly or through elected representatives,[29] and he supports the right of the people to create a new government when the old one, like the French monarchy, no longer serves its purpose and is beyond reform.[30] In each case

his arguments rest on the proposition that "the object of
all legitimate Government is the assertion and protection of the NATURAL RIGHTS OF MAN."[31] After
man has entered into society, these rights remain in their
"full integrity and vigor, if we except that *portion* . . .
which men mutually sacrifice for protection against each
other."[32] Natural rights are sanctioned not only by their
existence before the formation of society but by their
contribution to "general happiness" or "general interest."[33] All morality, "of which political principles form
only a part, . . . is . . . founded on a broad and general
expediency . . . into which reason has concentrated the
experience of mankind." However, this reasoned expediency does not, as Burke asserted, transmute natural
rights into continual compromises between good and
evil. The "general maxims" of justice and morality—including the "right to life, liberty, &c." and the right to
participate in government—are "founded on an utility
that is paramount and perpetual" and are so firmly established in experience that, although at any given time
some departure from them may seem expedient, the
precedent of *not* deviating outweighs "any utility that
may exist in the particular deviation."[34]

By 1796, when he visited Burke at Beaconsfield,
Mackintosh seems to have decided that unaided reason
may find it difficult to distinguish between perpetual
utility and dangerous freedoms.[35] In 1791, however, the
two men were still far apart regarding human "wants"
and the precedents of moral maxims and established
power. Burke occasionally uses the word *utility*, but his
idea of general happiness is considerably more restricted
and less substantial than that usually implied by the
term. He seems to consider it, as far as most men are
concerned, a state of virtue uncomplicated by the possession of material goods but palliated by confidence in an

after-life.[36] Whereas, for Mackintosh, *general* happiness implies not only political equality but a greater degree of economic equality than the English people enjoyed in 1791.[37] Between 1791 and 1796, however, the possibility of general happiness in this sense seemed, to many Englishmen, to have become more remote, while the people's aspirations came to look more like threats that called for the exercise of established authority. Or perhaps, as Hazlitt wrote about Burke and Mackintosh in *The Spirit of the Age*, "the influence exercised by men of genius and imagination" can overwhelm "those who have nothing to oppose to their unforeseen flashes of thought and invention, but the dry, cold, formal deductions of the understanding."[38]

Like Mackintosh, Paine and Godwin put their trust in reason. Both assert the extreme rationalist position that man is naturally good and reasonable, that the evils of society are due to "artificial causes," and that reform is a matter of letting nature do her work unhindered. The *Rights of Man* (1791, 1792) is a straightforward, lucid statement of this doctrine. Paine's common sense and pungent illustrations effectively undercut some of Burke's rhetoric, but Paine stops far short of Burke's comprehension of human behavior and the structure of society. If men are only given a chance to think reasonably, Paine argues, they will respect the rights of others. For these rights are sanctioned both by their "divine origin" and by their usefulness. Although men have formed governments to secure their natural rights, these rights are so strongly enforced by "a system of social affections . . . essential to . . . happiness" and by "the unceasing circulation of interest" that government becomes almost unnecessary.[39]

William Godwin also put his trust in mutual interest to minimize government or even do away with it entire-

ly. In 1793 Godwin replied to Burke with his *Enquiry
Concerning Political Justice, and Its Influence on Morals
and Happiness*. Briefly, Godwin argues that morality
and happiness (means and end, respectively) will be
consummated as men free themselves from the tyranny
of "institutions." Combining the doctrines of utility,
necessity, and the rights of man, Godwin finds promise
of rational and moral behavior and, therefore, of complete political and economic equality. Just as experience
relates cause and effect in the material world, Godwin
argues in *Political Justice,* so does it bind them together
by necessity in the mind itself, linking with certain propositions "the notion of preferableness or the contrary"
and directing, thereby, one's tendency to action.[40] Now,
since "men always act upon their apprehensions of preferableness," their actions will be virtuous and just—that
is, making for the general happiness—if by connecting
cause and effect they can see the preferableness of such
actions. But a higher law than any made by man is on
the side of justice. The immutable truth "that whatever
tends to produce a balance of [happiness and pleasure]
is to be desired, and whatever tends to a balance of [mis-
ery and pain] is to be rejected" is "founded in the nature
of things," for "vicious conduct is soon discovered to involve injurious consequences." If, therefore, man is allowed the free use of his reason—the faculty that enables
him to foresee consequences—he cannot but act toward
increasing the general happiness.[41]

Therefore men have no "rights" in the sense that
they may or may not choose a certain line of conduct,
for justice demands that they act always to increase the
general happiness; but since it is every man's duty to
employ himself to this end as best he may, everyone possesses, as the correlative of his neighbor's duties, certain
negative rights.[42] That is to say, as Godwin adds in his

second edition, "every man has a right to that, the exclusive possession of which being awarded to him, a greater sum of benefit or pleasure will result, than could have arisen from its being otherwise appropriated."[43] A quantity of food, clothing, and shelter necessary to keep a man alive will obviously contribute more to the general happiness by being awarded to a man who is entirely without food, clothing, or shelter than by being granted to one who is already adequately supplied with such property. Therefore, if the division of both labor and produce were made according to the demands of justice, everyone would have enough material goods at the cost of perhaps only half an hour's work per day.[44] Everyone would have the leisure necessary to further mental development, and consequently greater virtue, and would enjoy to a higher and ever higher degree the intellectual pleasures which give man his greatest happiness.

For progress toward such a society, truth must be made known through freedom of inquiry and freedom of expression.[45] Government must not perpetuate vice by preserving the distinction between rich and poor, for if a common stock of goods were built up through the labors of every citizen, "temptation would lose its power."[46] Along with private property, Godwin condemns such other "erroneous institutions" as marriage, religious conformity, oaths of fidelity, and laws for the suppression of libel. From all of these, government should withdraw its sanction and confine itself to the suppression of injustice against individuals and defense against invasion. As truths become more generally known and men more just, even the first of these will become hardly necessary and the second not a matter of maintaining a regular army but of a virtuous citizenry rallying to defend the common interest.[47]

Thus, according to Godwin, reason may come to

dominate passion and, as it does, man's concern for the
general welfare will replace selfishness in directing his
actions. The rational man, when confronted with alter-
natives, will choose the one tending to the greater increase of general happiness.

iii

The rational man—in a form a bit less rational than
Godwin made him out to be—also played an important
role in the defense of private property and free enter-
prise. The doctrine of laissez-faire affirmed the power of
reason to connect cause and effect and to determine behavior accordingly, but it designated "self-love" rather
than "benevolence" as the socially useful motive.[48]
Adam Smith had assumed a natural or inherent principle whereby the good of all results from the self-seeking
of each and had posited competitive effort for gain as the
basis of the economic system, inferring that a wise government should leave prices and wages to the law of supply and demand, and charity to the discrimination of
individuals. "Benevolence," narrowed in meaning to
the public or even private support of the poor, came to
be deprecated as interfering with free competition and
therefore as being "unjust."[49]

Malthus, replying to Godwin by elaborating a proposition from *The Wealth of Nations*,[50] stresses the resistance of passion to reason as well as the social efficacy of
self-love. Nature, according to the *Essay on Population*,
instead of making for a communistic anarchy of disinterested citizens, insures the division into economic classes,
with self-love as the ruling principle. Because the sexual
passion is "necessary" and "constant" and because the
food supply is limited—ultimately by the earth's produc-
tivity and actually by many intervening factors—popula-

tion will always increase to a point where, regardless of
human institutions, a marginal group must suffer want.
Malthus, however, does not content himself with finding
Godwin's "justice" inconsistent with "nature." Equal
distribution achieved through benevolence, he thinks,
is unnatural; but self-love may work for the happiness of
the group and bring about, if not the equitable distribution that would be deemed "just" among disinterested
men in a world of plenty, at least the approximation to it
that must be considered "just" among selfish beings in a
world of limited resources. In a community such as that
foreseen in *Political Justice,* where the communal stores
were open to all, population would increase so rapidly
that food production could not keep pace and scarcity
would soon result. "The spirit of benevolence" would
be "repressed by the chilling breath of want," and "the
mighty law of self-preservation" would soon restore "self-
love" to its "wonted empire." "Vice" as well as "misery"
would check population. Depredations from the common store would increase until "the laws of our nature"
were re-established, as the best remedies for overpopulation, private property, and the obligation of every man
to support his own children. A division into classes—
proprietors and laborers—would then be inevitable, for
those "born after the division of property" would have to
work for those who had more than enough for themselves.[51] Malthus' proposed course between "the advocate for the present order of things" and "the advocate
for the perfectibility of man and society" appealed especially to the moderate liberalism of the Whigs: with its
first number, in 1802, the *Edinburgh Review* began to
champion the principle of population; Samuel Parr, the
"Whig Johnson," rejoiced in Malthus' answer to Godwin; and Whig politicians applied Malthusian principles
to Poor Law legislation.[52] The *Quarterly Review,* al-

though for a time it rejected Malthus' principle, finally took comfort in this "incontrovertible answer to all sweeping reformers," considering it an advantage "to know . . . that the face of civilized society must always . . . be distinguished by the same features which it has hitherto borne; that our business therefore is to lessen or remove its blemishes, and to prevent their growing into deformities; but that we can no more organize a community without poverty, and its consequence, severe labour, than we can organize a body without natural infirmities, or add a limb to the human frame."[53]

The conception of benevolence as a moral obligation, revealed by reason, to grant the rights of others persisted in Godwin, Owen, and other radicals, but their writings had little practical effect in relieving poverty: Owen's proposed Villages of Cooperation, although safely within the laws of property, were rejected by the House of Commons' Committee on the Poor Laws, partly because they ran counter to the theories of political economy and partly because Owen had criticized the established system of property and wages.[54] On account of disgust with the "wild speculations" in revolutionary thought, Southey wrote in 1803, the "moral and political atmosphere" had become "unnatural and unwholesome";[55] and, according to Shelley in 1817, "gloom and misanthropy" were still "characteristic of the age."[56]

iv

Like others, Hazlitt doubted the possibility of "perfectly" rational and moral beings, but he continually defended the rights of man. He objected particularly to what he considered the narrow psychology and the low aims of political economy; for, he believed, the insistence that economic improvement depended on rational self-interest free from governmental interference was, practically, a denial of human rights and was, moreover, inimical to any improvement whatsoever. Hazlitt's explanation of human behavior limits society's approach to "perfection," but even a lesser degree of improvement, Hazlitt thought, could be realized only through increased virtue and benevolence.[57]

Since Hazlitt made his living as a journalist, his political writings deal principally with current or recent issues. In his "Project for a New Theory of Civil and Criminal Legislation" Hazlitt adds, as corollaries to his statement of natural rights, (1) that in order to protect the rights of the people "it is essentially requisite to extend the elective franchise," and (2) that since "no one acquires a right over another but that other acquires a reciprocal right over him . . ., it follows that combinations among labourers for the rise of wages are always just and lawful, as much as those among master manufacturers to keep them down."[58] However, these two issues—an extended franchise and the right to strike—are not Hazlitt's principal concerns in his political writings. Pitt's Combination Acts were to be repealed in 1824-1825, and the Reform Bill was to pass only two years after Hazlitt's death; but most of Hazlitt's political essays were written before 1820, when the defense of liberty was closer to the last ditch and the predominant issues were, rather, the divine right of kings and need for a change in the Poor Laws.

The pressures that Hazlitt resisted came to a focus within two fairly well-marked spans of time, which, if we except the "Project" (begun in 1792 and completed about 1828) and the *Life of Napoleon* (1828, 1830), include Hazlitt's principal works on politics. The first period—from the renewal of the war in 1803 to Whitbread's Poor Law Proposal in 1807—includes two of Hazlitt's major political pieces: *Free Thoughts on Public Affairs* (1806) and the *Reply to Malthus* (1807). During the twelve years that preceded Whitbread's proposal and Hazlitt's *Reply,* the problem of poverty had become increasingly acute. Deprived of his strip of common land by enclosure acts, forbidden by the Combination Acts to organize, denied representation in the Parliament that refused him a minimum wage, the agricultural laborer had to accept the hard charity of the Poor Laws. These provided that the difference between a subsistence wage and the wage paid by the farmer should be made up from the poor rates; thus the laborer—prevented by settlement laws from seeking higher wages elsewhere—lost all freedom of bargaining and became dependent on the parish. Those who could not work found an even worse fate in the squalor of the workhouse. After 1808, as war profits compensated landlords and farmers for feeding the poor and as manufacturing required more and more cheap labor, the problem of poverty received less attention until the time when the war ended, in 1815, and the foreign and domestic markets collapsed. The number of unemployed, further increased by discharged and pensionless soldiers and sailors, multiplied; wages and allowances to the poor were cut, while the Corn Laws, intended to perpetuate wartime prices, pushed the price of grain still higher. Harder times and renewed riots—and new countermeasures climaxed by the charge at Peterloo in 1819 —made the problems of poverty and civil liberty urgent ones again.[59] Thus the second period of Hazlitt's political writing, which may be dated 1814 to 1819, is delineated by the defeat of Napoleon and the restoration of the Bourbons abroad and by economic and political crises at home. During the remainder of his life, Hazlitt continued to write on politics. He was too devoted to liberty ever to stop defending it, but after 1820 his treatment of political issues became more detached and less polemical. An exception is the *Life of Napoleon,* which brings to a conclusion Hazlitt's long defense of the French Revolution. Hazlitt continued to see Napoleon as a symbol of political freedom, the enemy of legitimacy, and the last champion of the people. Although Hazlitt was casual about the future of most of his work, he evidently hoped that the *Life of Napoleon*—like the cause it stood for—would endure beyond his lifetime.[60]

Hazlitt's political writings—especially those from 1803 to 1807 and from 1814 to 1819—are linked by two principal themes: (1) the Napoleonic wars, with the correlative loss of civil liberty in England; and (2) the problem of poverty, with the accompanying loss of economic freedom. In writing on the second theme Hazlitt was, in a sense, opposing the revival of liberalism which had begun about the time of his first political essays. After about 1807 the issues between Whigs and Tories, which had been blurred since the early years of war, were sharpened as the Whigs embarked on a program of reform based on utilitarian principles. On the first theme, one may say, Hazlitt is arguing for natural rights; on the second, he is rejecting the principle of utility as a means of securing these rights.

With Pitt's death in 1806 and Fox in the office of Foreign Secretary, Hazlitt hoped for a modification of foreign policy. These hopes are expressed in *Free Thoughts on Public Affairs.* Hazlitt argues that France had been made a military power by her enemies—by "her convulsive struggles for existence, and in the cause of that liberty which was denied her!" He is equally concerned with liberty in England, and argues that the greatness of a nation depends not only on the courage of the soldier but on the determination of the citizen to resist tyranny.[61] These themes are elaborated in his

"Vetus" and "Illustrations of Vetus"—which were written, after the Battle of Leipzig, in 1813 and 1814—and in the *Life of Napoleon*. "Vetus" was Edward Stanley, who, writing in the *Times,* had demanded the unconditional surrender of France and the restoration of the Bourbons. The "principle that peace can never be made with an enemy," Hazlitt replies, "renders war on the part of that enemy a matter of necessary self-defence, and holds out a plea for every excess of ambition or revenge."[62] In opposition to an "exclusive patriotism . . . which professes to annihilate and proscribe the rights of others," Hazlitt supports a "reasonable" patriotism which remembers that people are "the creatures of circumstance, habit, and affection" or, in other words, that imagination has infused cultural and philosophical traditions with a persistent vitality which other nations must respect. Thus, writing about what might be called the first total war in Europe, Hazlitt anticipates some views on international affairs that have become more widely accepted since the most recent total war. Before the end of the eighteenth century, even with the growth of nationalism during and after the Renaissance, armies were small professional bodies, sometimes augmented by foreign mercenaries. The need of manpower to maintain a nation's economy limited both the quality and the quantity of military personnel, and those limitations restricted both the objectives and tactics of warfare to a rather small scale. The American and French Revolutions, however, were popular causes supported by peoples' armies. The peoples' physical and emotional involvement in warfare continued to increase, in general, during the next century and a half and culminated in the total wars of 1914-1918 and 1939-1945. The correlative policy of total defeat—not only the destruction of armies but the complete subjugation of the enemy's territory—also reached a consummation in the two World Wars. But, it has become increasingly evident, this policy can impose problems as difficult and dangerous as those which a war was originally fought to solve; and Western thought has more than begun to doubt whether, in the interests of international cooperation and peace, a nation may—in Hazlitt's words—make its "interests or prejudices the sole measure of right and wrong to other nations" or constitute itself the "sole arbiter of the empire of the world."[63]

In his *Free Thoughts,* his replies to Vetus, and his other political essays, Hazlitt's concept of human rights is the one he explains most fully in "A Project for a New Theory of Civil and Criminal Legislation." In defining the powers of government, he goes back to the limited political world of Hobbes. Like Hobbes, Hazlitt bases rights on the sanctity of the individual will. A right, he says in the "Project," is "not simply that which is good and useful in itself, but that which is thought so by the individual, and which has the sanction of his will as such." But because the will of another may inhibit the realization of this good, the principle of self-interest limits a person's right to that to "which, among a number of equally selfish and self-willed beings, he can lay claim, allowing the same latitude and allowance to others." It is "political justice" that "assigns the limits of these individual rights in society," and it is the function of government to see that these limits are enforced.[64]

This sounds very much like Hobbes and Locke. There is the same emphasis on self-preservation ("the right of society to make laws to coerce the wills of others, is founded . . . strictly on the right of self-defense or resistance to aggression") and the same insistence that this right is founded in nature (it is "inseparable from the order of the universe").[65] Hazlitt has not, like Burke, shifted the sanction of natural rights to the people's wants as determined solely by a morally solicitous ruling class or, like Mackintosh, Paine, Godwin, and Malthus, to the principle of utility. A right is not the reciprocal of a duty; it is not what is "best for the whole" but what is good in the individual's "own eyes."[66] Hazlitt believes that there cannot be legal action against drunkenness (as long as one keeps the peace), against unkindness to a wife (as long as one does not beat her or threaten her life), or against gambling (as long as one does not cheat).[67] In other words, "moral justice" is not identical with "political justice." It claims a "higher standard" than the calculation of consequences to one's self-interest. Rights are a matter of the individual will, limited by reason at a point where the limitation must be enforced by the government; morality is a matter of sympathetic identification with others and not subject to any legal enforcement within the circle of rights.[68] Hazlitt would agree with Burke that *morally* men are "never in a state of *total* independence of each other,"[69] but, within the circle prescribed by political justice, he would not make this mutual dependence a concern of the government.

But if "cold hearts, and contriving heads" are enough to define political justice, they are not enough to establish or maintain a free society.[70] Despite his acceptance of a Hobbesian kind of political justice, Hazlitt is not laying aside his usual reservations regarding either the selfish calculation of consequences or the abstract world of the understanding. A just society requires a moral context. Like Burke, Hazlitt refuses to keep politics within the framework of the *Leviathan,* just as he refused to keep reality within the psychological categories of Hobbes and Locke. The individualism of Hazlitt's political or economic man, as distinguished from that of his moral man, is strong and useful up to a point but incomplete. The social context within which a democratic society can come into existence and endure is a work of the imagination, requiring of the citizens a more complete kind of individualism: an internal harmony of reason and emotion which takes the external form of moral action.

Reason alone, without imaginative identification and unselfish sympathy, will not suffice. On this point, Hazlitt diverges from Mackintosh, Paine, and Godwin. Probably because he agrees with their conclusions, he has little to say about *Vindiciae Gallicae* or the *Rights of Man* beyond calling the former "stately and elaborate" and the latter "the only really powerful reply" to Burke's *Reflections*. But he also praises the "good taste, good sense, and liberal thinking" of an old friend who, having had the *Rights of Man* and the *Reflections* bound up in one volume, said that "both together, they made a very good book."[71] Hazlitt's witticism should not be taken too seriously, but it undoubtedly expresses something of his own opinion. Although he admires Paine's defense of the Revolution and apparently accepts Mackintosh's, he agrees with Burke that the people's welfare depends on a kind of virtue and wisdom that goes beyond a calculation of reciprocal interests or an instinct for social pleasure. Enlightened self-interest and a consequent identification of interests are enough to define the point at which individual rights should be limited for the sake of mutual protection, or to establish a "state of practical equality" in which the power of combination among the laborers would limit the employer's profits and thus assure adequate wages.[72] But political and economic equality, although *immediately* defined by the balance of selfish interests, can be achieved only if all citizens are secure in the exercise of certain rights;

and this security is possible only in a society where the individual recognizes the freedom of others as an end in itself and not merely as a means of serving his own interest or pleasure. Hazlitt does not, as Paine seems to, completely identify "the laws . . . of trade and commerce" with "the laws of nature."[73] In fact, he finds that "a commercial spirit," because it is self-interested, "is a very weak as well as dangerous substitute for a spirit of freedom."[74]

Similarly, Hazlitt could not accept Godwin's explanation of benevolence as something produced by an accurate calculation of consequences, nor could he share Godwin's expectation that this sort of calculation would produce a "perfect" society. The desire to increase another's happiness, says Hazlitt, is the result of "habit" and "circumstance" acting on the imagination. Since reason can be only a guide to morality, since one pursues a goal, either for himself or for another, only from "having an idea of it sufficiently warm and vivid to incite . . . an emotion of interest, or passion,"[75] man's benevolence must be limited well short of universality. Godwin "conceived too nobly of his fellows," placing "the human mind on an elevation, from which it commands a view of the whole line of moral consequences; and requir[ing] it to conform its acts to the larger and more enlightened conscience which it has thus acquired. He absolves men from the gross and narrow ties of sense, custom, authority, private and local attachment, in order that he may devote himself to the boundless pursuit of universal benevolence.[76] Hazlitt, therefore, did not foresee either the anarchy or the communism of *Political Justice*.[77] But if he believed that government, marriage, and private property would continue, he did not believe that these institutions, along with the limited resources of the earth, condemned a large part of the population to vice and misery. If Godwin conceived too nobly of his fellows, Malthus regarded them too basely. Up to a point, it is true, there is a certain similarity in Hazlitt's and Malthus's depreciation of the power of calculation to control the passions or the affections. Sexual passion is so strong, according to Malthus, that the good of society as a whole is too remote to enforce the preventive check if a couple are certain that society will support their child. Like Burke, Hazlitt was even more skeptical than Malthus of the *unaided* power of reason. Even the prospect of having to support one's own children, he replied in defense of the Poor Laws, will not enforce the preventive check unless "notions of comfort and decency" have fostered habits of prudence; for "the indulgence of [the sexual passion] is . . . governed almost entirely by circumstances, and may be said to be the creature of the imagination."[78] But, imaginatively integrated with habitually cultivated affections, a calculation of consequences may effectively control anti-social passions, including sexual desire, so that the increased control of passion is both cause and effect of moral progress.[79] Just because reason is not "the only infallible or safe rule of conduct," it does not follow "that it is no rule at all. . . . On the contrary . . . in proportion as we strengthen and expand this principle, and bring our affections and subordinate, but perhaps more powerful motives of action into harmony with it, it will not admit of a doubt that we advance to the goal of perfection, and answer the ends of our creation, those ends which not only morality enjoins, but which religion sanctions."[80]

The principal affection or passion which must combine with reason for the improvement of society is, of course, sympathy for others. In modern times, Hazlitt thought, the direction of speculative thought had diluted the affections and restricted the imagination. The modern philosophy had set the analytical temper of the times so that reformers were concerned too much with "dry formalities" and too little with "liberty and humanity."[81] The general indifference to the fate of the working classes effectively blocked the road to any improvement. Hazlitt believed that Malthus, through his attack on the Poor Laws, had formed "selfishness into a regular code," doing "all that was wanting to increase th[e] indifference and apathy" of the ruling classes toward the poor. While such prejudice subsisted "in its full force," Hazlitt was "almost convinced" that any serious attempt to relieve poverty would be likely to bind the poor in even more hopeless slavery.[82]

In Hazlitt's case against Malthus, the pattern of *Political Justice* is modified but still recognizable. Disinterestedness, subordinated by Malthus to self-love, becomes again a factor in improvement. Reason, depreciated by Malthus, collaborates with the proper affections to control anti-social passions. Once more nature surrenders the burden of evil to institutions. Although the "perfect" man does not figure in Hazlitt's predictions and although Godwin's communistic anarchy is curtailed to a state of "practical equality" with government, marriage, and private property, this practical equality must be fostered by disinterestedness, maintained by mastery over passion, and freed from "institutions" that artificially limit the production and distribution of goods and confirm selfish or irrational behavior.

v

But by disinterestedness Hazlitt does not mean a feeling prompted by identical interests or a natural instinct gratified by social intercourse; in his emphasis on compassion, on its primitive strength and current feebleness, and on its importance in socializing the general will, Hazlitt is closer to Rousseau than to Mackintosh, Godwin, or Paine. The fact that Rousseau, in Hazlitt's opinion, "did more towards the French Revolution than any other man" is of course enough to account for Hazlitt's admiration. But the manner in which Rousseau produced this effect also appealed to Hazlitt: "It was Rousseau who brought the feeling of irreconcilable enmity to rank and privileges, *above humanity,* home to the bosom of every man,—identified it with all the pride of intellect, and with the deepest yearnings of the human heart."[83] In other words, what Rousseau did was to bring about a supreme act of the imagination ordering and integrating the individual's thought and feeling into an active (and, according to Hazlitt, moral) hatred of rank and privilege.

Rousseau's description of democratic society lies in the tradition centering about natural rights. Like Locke, he believes that government depends on popular consent; and he goes further than Locke in providing constitutional means for expressing this consent.[84] However, he rejects self-interest as the bond of society, or as the basis of virtue and morality. Rousseau's state of nature, as he explains it in his *Discourse on Inequality* (1755), is a hypothetical, rather than historical, period before civil government was established.[85] It is marked by four stages. In the first of these man is merely an advantageously organized animal with a potential for self-improvement. He is free, equal, good, and stupid. His fundamental desire is for self-preservation, but his selfish desires are tempered by compassion. This stage ends as the human species increases in number, as human beings compete with other species for food, as this competition leads to attacks by animals, and as man—stimulated by competition with other animals and his fellow men—

begins to develop intelligence, that is, to *perfect* himself.[86] Unfortunately, as he becomes more "perfect," he
becomes more calculating and less compassionate, de-
veloping *amour-propre* as distinguished from his original *amour de soi-même*.[87] In the second stage, men unite
in herds for mutual protection; in the third, the family
becomes the unit of society and government; in the
fourth, the increasing wealth and power of some individuals subject the mass of people to a few.[88] This state
of affairs, like Hobbes' state of nature, leads to civil
government.

In the *Discourse on Inequality* Rousseau writes
grimly of civil government with its sacrifice of liberty
and conflict of interests. In the *Discourse on Political
Economy* (1758) and the *Social Contract* (1762) he admits at least the possibility of approximating natural
equality and freedom through recapturing something of
man's original compassion. Of course, Rousseau is not
suggesting a return to the condition of compassionate
though unreasoning animals, but it is interesting that he
describes the patriarchal stage as probably the happiest
and most stable epoch, before perfectibility has been
achieved at too great a cost of compassion.[89] Before men
reach the stage of civil government, morality develops
as something distinct from this primitive compassion,
which man often had to lay aside in order to redress the
injuries that had been done him.[90] But in a governed
state virtue requires, as a basic condition, the recapture
of compassion. In such a state virtue is the conformity
of the particular will with the general will, that is, the
direction of each individual will toward the common
good.[91] The general will is not merely the result of public deliberation—which may be seduced by private
interests—but a force that always works toward the preservation and welfare of the whole and of each part.[92] To

become part of the general will, individual wills must be socialized by compassion and enlightenment—through example, patriotism, personal security, education, civil religion, custom, and tradition.[93]

For Hazlitt the *vox populi* becomes the *vox Dei* under the qualifications that Rousseau applies to the general will.[94] As we have seen, Hazlitt believes that compassion is needed to direct individual wills toward the common good. In his own time he finds this quality, along with other emotions, sadly diminished by the progress of speculative thought and by the assumption that the enforcement of reason by self-love is the key to reform.[95] Hazlitt also believes that the people's will should be directed toward the public interest by education, by tradition, and by wise and virtuous leadership; but, more than Rousseau, he emphasizes the exchange of ideas as essential to this direction. ". . . by the aid of books and of an intercourse with the world of ideas," he points out in the *Life of Napoleon*, "we are purified, raised, ennobled from savages into intellectual and rational beings."[96] It is in his essay called "What is the People?" (1818) that he replies most directly to Burke. He is like Burke in believing that the voice of the majority is not necessarily an expression of the general will. "The will of the people" can attain "the general good as its end . . . as it is guided" not only "by popular feeling, . . . arising out of the immediate wants and wishes of the great mass of the people" but also "by public opinion, . . . arising out of the impartial reason and enlightened intellect of the community." But Hazlitt does not share Burke's distrust of the people or believe that their wills must constantly be restrained by a ruling class which possesses a monopoly of wisdom and virtue. Hazlitt does not count on "prescriptive prejudice and hereditary pretension" as a source of the self-fulfilling power of "moral imagination."[97] On the contrary, he agrees with Godwin that a powerful aristocracy not only gives rein to selfish ambition but blocks the "full and free development of public opinion" upon which the discovery of truth and the diffusion of knowledge and morality depend. The enlightened socialization of the people's will, beyond a concern for immediate wants, comes only with freedom from the tyranny that "exenterates us of our affections, blinds our understandings, [and] debases our imaginations." Hazlitt agrees with Burke that the solid wisdom of repeated experience and tradition is a safer guide in human affairs than naked reason and that the people need wise and virtuous leadership, but he believes that free inquiry is necessary to keep these resources open and available. Free inquiry promotes the discovery of truth, the preservation of traditional wisdom, and the rise of "natural genius" to leadership, so that public opinion comes to express "not only the collective sense of the whole people, but of all ages and nations, of all those minds that have devoted themselves to the love of truth and the good of mankind."[98] The greatest leaders have always risen from the people. "Even Burke was one of the people, and would have remained with the people to the last, if there had been no court-side for him to go over to."[99]

Hazlitt also resembles Rousseau in his belief that democracy demands whole human beings and that political action should reflect internal integration. Rousseau considered freedom more than a means of preserving the individual's physical welfare; he praised it as an end in itself.[100] Freedom is collective self-mastery in realizing the general will, and this self-mastery is good not only because it serves the general welfare by defining freedoms and restraints, but because it requires the kind of self-fulfillment that marks the essential difference be-

tween men and animals.[101] The animal mechanically
responds, whereas man knows himself free to acquiesce
or resist; and it is especially in his awareness of this liberty that he shows the spirituality of his soul. Hazlitt, as
we have seen, insists that the will is not the effect of mere
mechanical causes alone.[102] Its direction into moral action depends on an act of integrating imagination which
brings into harmony a sympathetic feeling for others and
the reasoned selection of the means to effect their welfare. A free society requires "the hand, heart, and head
of the whole community acting to one purpose, with a
mutual and thorough consent."[103] Hazlitt sees this kind
of society as growing organically and attaining what
Burke calls "symmetry with the order of the world," but
this will be an order that is imposed on its people's actions by their own virtue and wisdom, guided by the ac-
cumulated experience of "all ages and nations." Such a
view of democracy assumes whole human beings aspiring
toward—not only self-preservation—but self-realization.
Political freedom thus becomes not only a means to an
end but an end in itself, the culmination of a process by
which morally free citizens attain stature as human
beings.

vi

In *The Spirit of the Age* (1825) Hazlitt deals with
those forces in his own time that, he thinks, have prevented its men of genius or power from attaining this
sort of fulfillment. The three editions of *The Spirit of
the Age* that Hazlitt himself prepared for the press[104]
comprise twenty-three full-length "characters" and two
"short-notices." All of Hazlitt's subjects dealt in the
spoken or written word. Tooke, Mackintosh,
Brougham, Burdett, Lord Eldon, Cobbett, and Canning
are probably best classified as practicing politicians;

Jeffrey and Gifford as editors; and Bentham and Malthus as political economists. Edward Irving was a preacher. This leaves those who were primarily writers: Godwin, Coleridge, Scott, Byron, Southey, Wordsworth, Campbell, Crabbe, Moore, Leigh Hunt, Lamb, Washington Irving, and J. S. Knowles. All of these were men whose careers, if not complete, had pretty well defined themselves by 1825. *The Spirit of the Age* can hardly be classified as one of Hazlitt's political works, except in a very broad sense. Unlike *Free Thoughts,* the *Reply to Malthus,* and the *Political Essays* (collected in book form in 1819), it was not inspired by current political issues; but since politics are an important part of the milieu in which Hazlitt views his subjects, he has occasion to restate most of the ideas found in his earlier, more polemical works. Hazlitt's political ideas remain unchanged—as, indeed, they did throughout his life—but they are stated with more precision, economy, vividness, and tolerance. Even a number of old enemies, personal as well as political, fare better this time, as the age itself becomes the principal villain.

The book is mainly unified by the theme suggested in the title. "The Spirit of the Age," says Hazlitt, "was never more fully shown than in its . . . love of paradox and change, its dastard submission to prejudice and to the fashion of the day."[105] For Matthew Arnold, too, the age of the French Revolution represented a kind of paradox. At first sight Arnold finds it "strange that out of the immense stir of the French Revolution and its age should not have come a crop of works of genius" equal to that which came out of the Renaissance or the Age of Pericles; but unfortunately, he adds, the Revolution, by taking a "political, practical character" too soon, distinguished itself from those "disinterestedly intellectual and spiritual movements . . . in which the human spirit looked for its satisfaction in itself and in the increased play of its own activity."[106] Hazlitt offers a similar explanation for the failure of men of genius to realize their powers, although the immediate cause is not the practical direction of the Revolution but the inability of the age to deal with the forces of reaction. Hazlitt, like Arnold, believed that his age and its representative men were the victims of abstraction. He returns to the theme of "Why the Arts Are Not Progressive": the progress of science—of inquiry, experiment, and demonstration— checked the imagination and produced an age of materialism lacking in stable values.[107] The "preposterous rage for novelty" accounts for the success of that "popular declaimer" the Reverend Mr. Irving.[108] More grievously, the age has beset men of letters and affairs with forces against which it provided them no defense. The Lake poets were victims of both the love of novelty, which carried them too far from accepted standards of poetry, and a tyrannical government, which offered them rewards for their apostasy. "Genius stopped the way of Legitimacy, and therefore it was to be abated, crushed, or set aside as a nuisance." Those who did not give in were "assailed . . . by nicknames, by lies, by all the arts of malice, interest, and hypocrisy, without the possibility of their defending themselves."[109]

All the revolutionaries and reformers suffered some kind of reverse, but "the philosophers, the dry abstract reasoners" fared better than the literary men.[110] They found ready support, as the poets did not (before their apostasy at least), in a powerful political party and in the prevailing emphasis on intellect rather than feeling and imagination. But the abstraction of the modern philosophers was their weakness as well as their strength. Hazlitt admires the *Edinburgh Review* for its "spirit . . . of fair and free discussion" and its refusal merely "to serve the turn of a party." Its political opinions and critical decisions are "eminently characteristic of the Spirit of the Age." It "asserts the supremacy of the intellect"; it never appeals to "ignorance, or prejudice, or authority, or personal malevolence," but at the same time it relies "too little on the broad basis of liberty and humanity" and "enters too much into mere dry formalities." The shortcomings of the *Edinburgh Review* are most evident in its "unqualified encouragement" of "Mr. Malthus's system," a matter in which the *Quarterly*—whose "express object" is "to extinguish" the Spirit of the Age—has the advantage.[111] But the Tory leaders, although more emotional, are less disinterested than the Whig philosophers. As in Lord Eldon, the passions which carry the day against intellectual principles are "gross and immediate," or as in Southey, "the indulgence of vanity, of caprice, or prejudice" wins out over "abstract principle."[112] It is from "slothful and self-willed prejudices" that Scott opposes the Spirit of the Age.[113] In neither Whig nor Tory are thought and feeling disinterestedly integrated in the kind of imaginative activity required by genius, whether literary or political. All of Hazlitt's characters suffer from some degree of abstraction, which Hazlitt traces to the age in which they lived. The Spirit of the Age, obviously, is not just one thing: it is change in general, and reform in particular; it is the rage for novelty but paradoxically it is also a return to prejudice; it is self-love and disinterestedness; it is the clash between change and reaction which was unresolved in individuals as well as in public affairs. Hazlitt does not state a comprehensive definition; but he shows how selfish preoccupation or narrow rationalism, enforced by external pressures, blocked the imagination and prevented able men from fulfilling their powers.

III

The Creative Imagination

> . . . the imagination is that faculty which represents objects, not as they are in themselves, but as they are moulded by other thoughts and feelings, into an infinite variety of shapes and combinations of power.—"On Poetry in General" (1818).

IN 1812 HAZLITT BEGAN his journalistic career as a Parliamentary reporter for the London *Morning Chronicle,* and in the following year he was supplying that paper with essays on the stage, books, and art as well as on politics and philosophy. As early as 1814 Francis Jeffrey recognized his accomplishment as a critic by inviting him to contribute to the *Edinburgh Review;*[1] and for the rest of his life Hazlitt continued, at frequent intervals, to write on literature and art for leading newspapers and magazines. It is in his essays on art and literature that Hazlitt most fully explains his views of the imagination and its effects.

i

The high estimate of the imagination which Hazlitt shares with other Romantic critics consummates a long period of reassessment for this faculty. By Hazlitt's time, the word *imagination* frequently meant a faculty which not only achieves a moral identification with others but perceives truth and reality: a creative faculty which,

enabled by intense feeling to see otherwise unrevealed
similitudes, selects, molds, and unifies concrete particulars to represent essential truth and provide aesthetic
pleasure. The skeleton of this definition, which was to
be fleshed by the increasingly high regard of Romantic
critics and poets, is the proposition—frequently offered
by Hobbes, Hartley, and others—that recollected images
are intuitively combined according to cause and effect,
resemblance, contiguity, and other kinds of previous
association.[2]

In describing this process Hobbes uses the terms
imagination and *fancy*, both of which—and the faculties
they designate—made but a poor showing in the light of
the seventeenth century's new science. *Wit*, when it
meant the same thing as *fancy*, underwent a similar depreciation. Hobbes principally thinks of imagination as
mere imaging and calls it "nothing but decaying sense."
A "compound imagination," or combination of separate
images, is "properly but a fiction of the mind." The faculty that observes similitudes Hobbes calls "fancy" or
"good wit." This is a component of man's "natural wit"
(which Hobbes considers an admirable complex of faculties), but unless controlled by judgment—the faculty
that perceives differences—fancy becomes "one kind of
madness." Hobbes speaks out for literal, denotative language, and classifies metaphors with "senseless and ambiguous words" as false and misleading.[3] Locke makes a
similar distinction. "Wit and fancy" (both terms, in
this context, meaning the faculty of seeing similitudes)
give "pleasure and delight"; but when it comes to "dry
truth and real knowledge," the "figurative speeches" of
fancy do "nothing else but . . . insinuate wrong ideas,
move the passions, and thereby mislead the judgment;
and so indeed are perfect cheats. . . ."[4] As far as science
and, in general, speculative thought are concerned,

Hobbes and Locke are of course right in their insistence on literal terms and in ignoring the powers of figurative language to state the truth. There are other areas of human experience, however, which only metaphor can reduce to statement and which therefore require, for their description, a synthesizing faculty which perceives similitudes. A "moral value" can be named but not given "reality" in literal, denotative language. Such a reality is a state of mind that necessarily includes emotion. To express or evoke this state of mind, language must carry a charge of feeling, which it acquires by escaping its literal boundaries, usually through comparison, stated or implied. Of course, some sort of control is needed to keep the comparing faculty from running wild. Pope finds "wit" and "judgment" often "at strife";[5] and Dr. Johnson, although he can praise imagination for recalling and combining vivid pictures, often deprecates it as an "idle," "wild," "vain," or "licentious and vagrant faculty" that "has always endeavoured to baffle the logician, to perplex the confines of distinction, and burst the inclosures of regularity."[6] William Duff and Alexander Gerard represent a later stage in the history of the word *imagination* in which the imagination has come to be considered definitely superior to judgment in the constitution of genius; but they still expect the "cool, attentive, and considerate" faculty of judgment to "counterbalance . . . the rambling and volatile power of imagination."[7]

The depreciation of the synthesizing or combining faculty below the analyzing or dividing one seems to have been caused largely by the seventeenth century's scientific emphasis on close observation and analysis. But if Hobbes degraded imaginative compounds or "fictions," he undermined reason as well, and furnished later writers with grounds for elevating the imagination.

For reason, he says, depends on language, and language is a further step from reality than sensation or imagination. All language withdraws from sensory experience; and since reasoning requires general terms in general propositions, its language is especially abstract. Reasoned language, in Hobbes' sense, is not only abstract but confined by strict definition, each word, ideally at least, being distinguished from every other and cleared from the overtones of passion. A "reasoned" statement, therefore, could deal with only a part of human experience. For Samuel Johnson reason continued to be the comprehensive kind of faculty that it was during the Renaissance, but among many of his contemporaries, and more generally later, it was reduced to the merely analytical and deductive faculty, excluding emotion, empirical wisdom, and immediate insight. Thus shorn of emotion, it often seemed an insufficient guide to moral action. Even that relentless reasoner, William Godwin, admitted as much.[8] On the other hand, as we have seen, imagination and feeling became increasingly recognized as allies against selfishness.[9] Imagination had long been closely linked with emotion. Hobbes himself observed that "men's passions" are useful to "celerity of imagining"; and in the eighteenth century emotion was increasingly valued as accelerating, directing, and unifying the train of associated images that enter into an imaginative synthesis.[10]

Imagination also became a means of knowing, as Addison puts it, the "Wonders of [divine] Creation." Addison traces the "Pleasures of the Imagination" principally to "the Sight [or recollection] of what is *Great, Uncommon, or Beautiful*." Among these three sources of pleasure, the first two also furnish the observer with insight into the nature of the universe or with new impressions of its contents. Contemplating "Great or Unlimited" vistas is equivalent, in providing a delightful sense of purpose and value, to the contemplation of God himself; and the "*new* or *uncommon* raises a Pleasure in the Imagination, because it fills the Soul with an agreeable Surprise, gratifies its Curiosity, and gives it an Idea of which it was not before possest." The enjoyment of the beautiful is also connected with the discovery of truth, but less closely. By beauty Addison seems to mean (1) the attractiveness of a member of the opposite sex which tempts "all Creatures . . . to multiply their Kind"; (2) the variety of light and color with which God renders "the whole Creation more gay and delightful"; and (3) a regular pattern in a multiplicity of parts. The third kind of beauty discloses the "Effect of Design" in nature as well as art; but the first two kinds lack objective reality. ". . . every different Species . . . has its Different Notions of Beauty [in the oposite sex, and] Light and Colours, as apprehended by the Imagination, are only Ideas in the Mind. . . ."[11]

All these pleasures of the imagination and the accompanying revelation of divine immensity, purpose, and order proceed immediately from the objects observed, without any act of ratiocination. They employ the mind less seriously than the understanding does and are "easie to be acquired." The pleasures derived from works of art representing the Great, the Uncommon, and the Beautiful are principally of the same kind as those offered by natural objects themselves, but they may be supplemented by the pleasure of comparing a work of art with the object it represents. Addison distinguishes between "Primary Pleasures of the Imagination" entirely proceeding "from such Objects as are before our Eyes," and "Secondary Pleasures of the Imagination" flowing from images that are either recalled by memory or called up by "Paintings, Statues, Descriptions, or any

like Occasion." Some of the pleasures of the latter sort
arise from comparing the representation with the thing
represented. The *"final Cause"* of this pleasure probably lies in our "Searches after Truth," which are thus
furthered but not, of course, without involving the understanding as well as the imagination. The pleasure of
finding "Congruity or Disagreement," Addison grants,
might be "more properly called the Pleasure of the Understanding," since it involves abstracting and comparing as well as imaging. Thus Addison further elevates
the pleasures of the imagination by joining them with
the more "refined," "more preferable," and more "serious" pleasures of the understanding and with the kind
of "Knowledge or Improvement in the Mind of Man"
that these pleasures accompany.[12] These pleasures of
the understanding, in their conjunction with the "easie"
pleasures of the imagination, take on an aspect of immediacy, but Addison is not very specific on this point.

To find the operations of the understanding rendered immediate as part of the truth-finding process, we
may turn to Sir Joshua Reynolds. In Discourse XIII in
his *Discourses on Art* Reynolds describes that "sound
reason"—as distinguished from "partial reasoning" or
"cold consideration"—which "does not wait for the slow
process of deduction, but goes at once, by what appears
a kind of intuition, to the conclusion." In Discourse III
Reynolds had pointed out that the process by which the
artist isolates "ideal beauty" from the accidents of time
and place and thus captivates the imagination entails a
long apprenticeship of "observing the works of nature,
... skill in selecting, and ... care in digesting, methodiz-
ing, and comparing our observations." In Discourse XIII
Reynolds finds that this process culminates in a "sagaci-
ty" which acts immediately to distinguish what is natural and true. For Reynolds, the imagination appears to

be the faculty which is "captivated" or "delighted" by
the embodiment of ideal beauty and which immediately
recognizes its truth, whereas the faculty which enables
the artist to distinguish and embody the ideal is *"sound
reason"* (the adjective being necessary to distinguish
this kind of reason from the analytical variety).[13]

Reynolds does not hand "sound reason" over to the
creative imagination, but this next step in elevating the
imagination is taken in Abraham Tucker's *The Light of
Nature Pursued* (1768-1778), of which Hazlitt published
an abridgment in 1807.[14] All the faculties of the mind,
says Tucker, or all the "modes or species of perception,"
can be reduced to two general classes: imagination and
understanding, both "acquired by use and practice."
The former comprehends "every representation to the
mind, whether of things real or fantastical, either brought
into view by some sensation, or starting up of their own
accord." When some of these ideas are "engaging"
enough to attract repeated attention to themselves, the
mind may single them out for special attention. Some
imagined idea, for instance, may cause a person to try to
satisfy his curiosity about it and to trace out the chain of
cause and effect leading to its actual or desired existence.
In this case the understanding goes to work. For Tucker, imagination comprises the images themselves and
their concatenation in free, spontaneous association,
whereas the understanding is the power of deliberately
stopping or directing the flow of images.[15] Just as the
understanding grows out of the imagination, the understanding returns its findings to the imagination. That is,
when a conclusion that has been "worked out by consideration of various particulars" becomes spontaneous
through habit "without the suggestion of any proof," its
recurrence is an act of imagination.[16] "For what occurs spontaneously, and readily, whether this be owing

to the vividness of impression, habit, or any other cause, I call a movement of the imagination; and what requires pains, art, or contrivance, to bring to light, is . . . an act of understanding." Thus, the understanding's comprehension of cause and effect and other relationships builds discrimination into the imagination, so that the imagination provides an immediate awareness of "self-evident truth."[17] Similarly, in 1774, John Ogilvie included "the faculty of reason" in the imagination's "instantaneous perception" of a subject suitable for imitation. In approving this choice, the reason acts "without any regular series of argument [or any interposition of the understanding] in the same manner as the eye . . . observes with ease that harmony which ariseth from a general correspondence of parts in some magnificent structure."[18]

The imagination's awareness of truth, whether in nature or in art, obviously depends on the immediate impact of the particular. "No description, that rests in generals, can be good," said Blair in 1783. "For we can conceive nothing clearly in the abstract; all distinct ideas are formed upon particulars."[19] In the older tradition, the concrete was considered symbolic of the universal: the meaning of physical objects could be inferred by reason. According to Addison's appraisal of the imagination, concrete details have an immediately pleasant effect, which may be inseparable from a feeling of divine presence and order but which, on the other hand, may comprise only a "pleasing Delusion."[20] Other critics likewise dissociated the pleasure-giving power of sensory details from the communication of knowledge.[21] The particular regained its symbolic power through association. As Tucker points out, habitual association can condition the mind to an immediate awareness of truth in certain combinations of particulars. Particulars in a

work of art or literature, therefore, came to be valued
not only for their pleasing or striking effects but for initiating trains of association established by general experience and providing, thereby, a recognition of truth.

Association also explains the "newness" of works of
the imagination. Johnson and Burke had agreed that
"the imagination is incapable of producing any thing ab-
solutely new; it can only vary the disposition of those
ideas which it has received from the senses."[22] Addison
had not been consistent about the creative power of the
imagination; or, rather, he had recognized that imagination has the power of pleasing by the exactness of its representation and also by giving a "Landskip . . . more
vigorous touches" and thus getting "the better of Nature." A poet pleases by providing "a more complex
Idea" of an object than we already have or by raising
only "such Ideas as are most apt to affect the Imagination."[23] Later writers go farther in ascribing creative
power to the imagination and in making the creative
imagination essential to genius. For imagination, operating in a state of emotion, likens an object to something
associated with the attendant feeling and thus molds
image into metaphor. Even when the imagination "only
exhibits simple ideas which have been derived from the
senses," says Gerard, "it confers something original upon
them. . . ." It presents "these ideas, not as copies but as
originals."[24] In more complex combinations, the "imagination is still more inventive. . . . It can transpose, vary,
and compound our perceptions into an endless variety of
forms, so as to produce numberless combinations that
are wholly new." The components of such a combination are not merely rearranged but are organically unified by the feeling that directs their selection. ". . . a
passion . . . always moulds those [ideas] which are intro-
duced, into its own likeness, or into a form agreeable to

itself, and it suffers none to enter which are not suscept-
ible of this form."[25] Coalesced by congruent associations, the particulars attain the distinctive unity of a
"new creation."[26] Since early in the century English
criticism had linked genius with newness or originality,
especially as distinguished from mere correctness, close
imitation, or adherence to narrow rules.[27] As imagination became the faculty responsible for new creations, it
was, as Duff testifies, "universally acknowledged" as the
"quality of all others most essentially requisite to the
existence of Genius."[28]

ii

Thus, since Hobbes' time, the imagination had acquired new powers. Most of these Hazlitt recognizes as
early as 1805 in his *Essay on the Principles of Human
Action,* where he describes the imagination as a faculty
which, when conditioned by sympathy and habitual reason, immediately charges particulars with thought and
emotion to create—not fantasy—but truth and reality.
In his critical essays written between 1814 and his death
in 1830, Hazlitt expands this definition to include other
powers attributed to the imagination by eighteenth-
century writers on the subject. René Wellek has pointed
out that Hazlitt owes little to Coleridge for either critical principles or critical method and that, in his empiri-
cism and emotionalism, he is closer to Wordsworth.
"The prefaces to *Lyrical Ballads,* though rarely referred
to, are clearly basic texts from which much of Hazlitt's
own theory is derived."[29] Undoubtedly Hazlitt's *Essay*
and the 1800 Preface share a number of assumptions regarding habitual thought and feeling, sympathetic
identification, and association in a state of excitement;
but the elaborate arguments of the *Essay* could owe little, if anything, to Wordsworth's fragmentary explana-

tion of these phenomena.[30] Both the 1800 and the 1815 Prefaces, however, may have influenced Hazlitt's later work.

Whereas the *Essay* and Hazlitt's political writings stress the moral, sympathizing quality of the imagination, his critical essays emphasize its creative, truth-finding power. A good deal of what Hazlitt says about the imagination applies equally to his two favorite arts, painting and poetry. He thinks of either a painting or a poem as rendered true and natural by the "heightenings of the imagination," which provide an "imitation of nature" rather than a copy. In both arts he attributes the highest excellence to imagination stimulated by intense feeling; but although he had been a painter himself, although in one passage he disclaims giving "any preference" to either painting or poetry, and although in another he prizes "the pleasures of painting" more than those of writing, he generally favors poetry over painting because it gives greater scope to the imagination. "Painting embodies what a thing contains in itself: poetry suggests what exists out of it, in any manner connected with it. But this last is the proper province of the imagination."[31] This province is best explored, therefore, in Hazlitt's literary criticism, although his essays on painting, and on sculpture as well, must not be overlooked. Particularly useful are "On Imitation," "On Gusto," and "Why the Arts Are Not Progressive" in *The Round Table* (1817); "On Poetry in General"[32] and "On Shakspeare and Milton" in *Lectures on the English Poets* (1818); and "On Genius and Common Sense" and "On Certain Inconsistencies in Sir Joshua Reynolds's Discourses" in *Table-Talk* (1821).

Hazlitt defines imagination as "that faculty which represents objects, not as they are in themselves, but as they are moulded by other thoughts and feelings, into an infinite variety of shapes and combinations of power." All the business of life, all its "reality," Hazlitt points out, is made up from perceptions shaped "according to our wishes and fancies." But beyond the "mere delineation of natural feelings," poetry requires the "heightenings of the imagination." In a state of intense feeling the poet's imagination finds otherwise unrevealed similitudes. The imagination is always an "*associating* principle." Directed by emotion, the imagination ranges through established associations to link one image with another that will convey the poet's feeling to the audience. "Let an object . . . be presented to the senses in a state of agitation or fear—and the imagination will . . . convert it into the likeness of whatever is most proper to encourage the fear."[33] An "image" is distinguished from a merely descriptive detail by suggesting a resemblance—or multiple resemblances—to something else, and thus building up a charge of emotion.[34] Not held back by the "limits of sense" or the "distinctions of understanding . . . , the poetical impression of any object . . . strives to link itself to some other image of kindred beauty or grandeur," the resulting coalescence becoming infinitely richer as additional resemblances suggest themselves.[35] Hazlitt's illustrations in "On Poetry in General" are not unlike Wordsworth's in his 1815 Preface, but are less explicitly categorized and explained. The linking of images may be relatively simple as in the metaphor Hazlitt quotes from *Cymbeline*, where Iachimo's feeling for Imogen transmutes the "flame o' th' taper" into the likeness of a bowing admirer;[36] or it may construct a more elaborate "combination of power" like Lear's identification of himself with the heavens or like the passage from *Antony and Cleopatra* (cited not in "On Poetry in General" but in a footnote to the *Essay*), where a despairing Antony sees himself in a series of evanescent cloud-pictures at the close of day.[37]

The "poetic impression" of an object attains a kind of truth that Hazlitt could not find in any of Hobbes' and Locke's particular or general ideas. For one thing, it captures the flux of actual experience, which refuses to be confined to any set of particulars or to any level of abstraction.[38] The imagination is never static, but—for both the poet and his audience—it exists in a dynamic, multiplying interplay of image, thought, and feeling. It enables poetry to put "a spirit of life and motion into the universe . . . [to] describe the flowing, not the fixed."[39] In this respect, poetry surpasses painting not only by showing an object in the light of different moods but also, because poetry includes the dimension of time, by comprising a variety of actions and—even within the same character—a number of shifting characteristics.[40] This flux is different from the "confusion" and "contradiction" of Hobbes' and Locke's particular and abstract ideas, which in actual experience slide helplessly from one level of abstraction to another. As emotion becomes more intense, the poet's imagination associates more "consistently" as well as "strongly," selecting and modifying his materials to bring them into a harmonious pattern that is a controlled "imitation" of nature and not a confused copy.[41] This harmonizing of sensory materials by strong emotion extends to the sound effects of poetry as well as to the figures of speech. When an object stimulates "passion" and therefore the imaginative process, this process sustains itself not only by modifying other objects according to a dominant feeling but also by regulating the sounds that express this emotion. Hazlitt recognizes that emotion naturally leads to rhythmical utterance, but his case for meter does not stop here. Meter is part of imitation. It results "wherever a move-

ment of imagination or passion is impressed on the
mind, by which it seeks to prolong and repeat the emotion, to bring all other objects into accord with it, and to
give the same movement of harmony, sustained and continuous, or gradually varied according to the occasion, to
the sounds that express it." Under such circumstances
"the music of language" answers to "the music of the
mind."[42] It is by linking feeling with image, image with
image, and feeling with sound, that the imagination
fuses "the world of thought within us, . . . with the world
of sense without us."[43]

The great poet or artist, however, does not see objects merely through the medium of either transitory or
exclusively personal feelings. Even in day-to-day experience we have associated various thoughts and feelings,
and degrees of pain or pleasure, with certain signs, so
that, when these signs recur, we find them a spontaneous
and reliable guide to practical decisions. Although a
whole "series of association" may have originally linked a
"circumstance" with the "state of mind" which its recurrence induces, "the mind drops the intermediate links,
and passes on rapidly and by stealth to the more striking
effects of pleasure or pain which have naturally taken the
strongest hold of it." By repeated experience and "the
law of association," the mind "forms a series of unpremeditated conclusions on almost all subjects that can be
brought before it. . . ." In phrasing reminiscent of
Reynolds', Hazlitt calls this intuitive power "tacit reason," and like Tucker he attributes it to the imagination. This "common-sense" is what Hazlitt describes, in
the *Essay,* as "reasoning imagination." It is the result of
"ingrafting reason on feeling," and therefore it will
"bear the test and abide the scrutiny of the most severe
and patient reasoning."[44] Conditioned by thoughtful
experience, the associating imagination is not what Dr.

Johnson called a "licentious and vagrant faculty" needing judgment to correct it, but a faculty that already embraces judgment. Analogous to "common-sense" but differing from it in "strength and depth of feeling" and in the resulting insight, is the power of genius to link ideas according to firmly established associations and thus to intuit truth.[45]

iii

Hazlitt calls genius "originality" and describes it as "for the most part, *some strong quality in the mind, answering to and bringing out some new and striking quality in nature.*" Emotionally aroused by this quality, the man of genius shapes nature anew, but "not to shew us what has never been, . . . but to point out what is before our eyes and under our feet, though we have no suspicion of its existence."[46] Every work of genius is unique; but it must also be true, and its truth must be immediately recognized and enjoyed. Too much, I think, can be made of Hazlitt's aphorism that the "truth is not one, but many. . . ." Hazlitt also says that it is the "form of truth . . . not its essence, [that] varies with time and circumstances."[47] The essence of truth depends on common experience. For Hazlitt, as for Wordsworth, the "object" of poetry is "truth, not individual and local, but general, and operative; not standing upon external testimony, but carried alive into the heart by passion; truth which is its own testimony, which gives competence and confidence to the tribunal to which it appeals, and receives them from the same tribunal."[48] The poet's immediate perceptions embody truth provided that experience has conditioned his perception to include "tacit reason" and that he has shared, through sympathetic identification, the experience of others. Hazlitt further agrees with Wordsworth that the poet must give "im-

mediate pleasure" through generally moving materials.[49]
The reader responds to a poem by an act of the imagination initiated by emotion-charged images, but this creative act will not get under way unless reader and poet
share the same associations. Genius, therefore, cannot
be self-centered; it must stamp natural objects not merely with the artist's "individual interest" but with the
"character" of mankind in general.[50]

One of Hazlitt's principal criteria for poetic excellence is the poet's ability to reach beyond his merely
personal interests to matters of general concern. Too
many of his contemporaries, it seemed to Hazlitt, wrote
only about themselves, but the writer of great poetry
brings, to the moment of coalescence, feelings conditioned by sympathetic identification with others. As
Hazlitt argues in the *Essay,* a readiness to share another's
feelings may be fixed by "habit, or association."[51] A
similar loss of self, habitually encouraged, is necessary if
the poet is to know the common patterns of human experience. "Those who have the largest hearts have the
soundest understandings; and he is the truest philosopher who can forget himself."[52] It is only when the poet
has been habitually sympathetic with others that the
language of poetry attains and communicates the highest
truth. Shakespeare and Milton acquired "their power
over the human mind" because, unhampered by egotism, they developed a "deeper sense than others of what
was grand in the objects of nature, or affecting in the
events of human life."[53] This perceptive "sympathy,"
or loss of self, extends even to inanimate objects. The
painter " 'sees into the life of things' . . . by . . . the im-
proved exercise of his faculties, and an intimate sympathy with nature."[54] By scrutinizing many works of art
as well as natural objects "with an eye to [themselves],
not merely to his own vanity or interest," the artist ac-

customs himself to recognize order in what would otherwise be a confusion of blurred details.[55]

Hazlitt agrees with Johnson and Reynolds that "it is the business of poetry, and indeed all works of imagination, to exhibit the species"—but it must do this *"through the individual."* Hazlitt frequently objects to Reynolds' argument "that the perfection of art consists in giving general appearances without individual details."[56] Here Hazlitt is taking issue with Reynolds on several points: (1) the degree of generalization permissible in the essential quality of a work of art, (2) the use of particulars to represent or suggest that quality, and (3) the manner in which a work of art pleases. Reynolds places beauty in a "central form" toward which "Nature is continually inclining." This "ideal" form is ascertained by abstracting from all the individual forms of a species and thus freeing it from any eccentricities or accidents.[57] Hazlitt agrees that a work of art should express "abstractions"; on the other hand, he says, these should not be of "human nature in general" but "of some single quality or customary combination of qualities."[58] The possibility of a central form representing a class within a species is not, of course, one that Reynolds overlooks.[59] Nor does he (for he cannot) rule out all particulars. He would retain those "great characteristick distinctions, which press strongly on the senses, and therefore fix the imagination."[60] But he does insist that a "minute attention" to particulars, with neither selection nor modification, is incompatible with the "grand style of Painting," which represents "the invariable, the great, and general ideas . . . fixed and inherent in universal Nature."[61] Hazlitt, on the other hand, finds the universal in the particular, but it is the particular made representative by being seen under special circumstances of emotion, conditioned sympathy, and in-

sight. This does not imply any difference from Reynolds
in the immediacy of the truth-recognizing process (at
least as Reynolds describes it in Discourse XIII) but in
what this process includes: for Reynolds, "sound reason," although carefully distinguished from "cold calculation," is still a process that corrects the model while
abstracting toward a central form; while according to
Hazlitt, the artist, through a properly conditioned imagination, immediately recognizes the model that best
expresses some abstract quality or "ideal" and then intensifies each sign of that quality, "imbuing every part
with that one predominant character to the utmost" and
only stopping short of caricature or the "loss of humanity."[62] It is difficult, especially in view of Discourses XI
and XIII, to keep these two processes and their results
entirely distinct. However, Hazlitt distinguishes the ultimate products of Reynolds' process as having lost,
along with minute particulars, "all expression, character,
and discrimination of form and colour," whereas a su-
perlative painter "approaches . . . reality [by] leaving out
[only] such particulars as are inconsistent with the preconceived idea . . . and retaining all such [even the most
minute] as are striking, probable, and consistent."[63] For
both Reynolds and Hazlitt the spectator's aesthetic pleasure is the result of an immediate impact on the imagination.[64] Reynolds attributes this pleasure to the
spectator's having been accustomed to the ideal form
which the imagination recognizes as complete in the assemblage of "great characteristick distinctions." Hazlitt
also recognizes "custom, or the association of ideas" as a
source of pleasure; but the particulars that initiate the
trains of associated ideas must be those, great or small,
which the artist has perceived in a state of intense feeling
and not details which have been emotionally discharged
through an intermediate process of abstraction. These

latter, says Hazlitt, would "leave nothing for his imagination, or the imagination of the spectator to work upon."[65]

iv

The pleasures of the imagination which Hazlitt finds stemming from particulars may be traced, mainly, to the "four principal sources" of beauty listed by Tucker: "composition, succession, translation, and expression." Each of Tucker's four categories involves association and thus relates the enjoyment of art to the audience's previous experience. The elements of "composition"—"symmetry, proportion, and order"—are pleasing because "they consist in the correspondence of objects with the trains of our imagination," which, in turn, are derived from previous experience. That is, we enjoy certain patterns when the mind "can range over them by paths to which it has been accustomed"; we appreciate the "regularity in a fine building," only if we are accustomed to discerning this kind of symmetry and proportion. "Succession," or "a variety of objects succeeding each other," is pleasing because it prevents an "insipid" or "cloying" monotony; yet variety must not degenerate into mere novelty and thus destroy all perception of order; for "the mind feels an awkwardness and irksomeness" in receiving entirely new assemblages.[66] Hartley goes even farther than Tucker in offering association to explain the pleasures of both "uniformity and variety in conjunction." He accounts for those partly by "association with the beauties of nature; partly by that with works of art; and with the many conveniences which we receive from the uniformity and variety of the works of nature and art."[67] Tucker's third source of pleasure is "translation," by means of which a person may seem to us more beautiful or hand-

some because his face suggests qualities that we have
found pleasing in another. Next comes "expression,"
Tucker's "fourth and most plentiful source of beauty."
This is the capability of particulars, especially "turns of
feature," to convey amiable, moral, or otherwise agreeable qualities of a person. These pleasures of expression
vary with the viewer's stock of associations, such as determined by his sex and experience.[68] Thomas Reid and
Archibald Alison are better known than Tucker for at-
tributing expression to emotion-producing associations,
but whereas Hazlitt had abridged Tucker, there is no
evidence that he had read either Reid's *Essays on the Intellectual Powers of Man* (1785) or Alison's *Essays on
the Nature and Principles of Taste* (1790).[69]

Although Hazlitt's aesthetic is more objective than
Tucker's, it still depends on various kinds of association.
It makes the audience's experience, extrinsic to the work
of art, something that art both exploits and illuminates.
Hazlitt only infrequently suggests (and mainly in his
practical criticism rather than in his statement of theory)[70] that he finds any sort of order peculiar to the work
of art itself. He is not ordinarily inclined to distinguish
among beauty, truth, and nature: in fact, he calls it "affectation" to separate the "*ideal* in art . . . from the study
of nature. . . . To the genuine artist, truth, nature,
beauty, are almost different names for the same thing."[71]
For Hazlitt the word *nature* includes everything that
exists, human or otherwise; and, although he may occasionally separate nature from any "interference of human power and contrivance,"[72] he ordinarily uses the
word to designate natural objects as perceived by someone and therefore put into some kind of order within
that person's mind or, quite often, as perceived, selected,
and molded by the artist. Sometimes, as we have seen,
Hazlitt calls this artistically ordered view an "imitation

of nature." This kind of order is not, however, unique
to art. A close scrutiny of the object itself can disclose
the same pleasing harmony. Like Addison, Hazlitt finds
that natural objects and their representation produce
the same kind of pleasure, which art may increase by
adding an element of excitement and by providing an
opportunity to compare the object with its representation. A work of art or a natural object, Hazlitt adds,
gives pleasure by linking ideas in a design that the observer's previous experience has prepared him to discern
and therefore to enjoy. "The learned amateur is struck
with the beauty of the coats of the stomach laid bare, or
contemplates with eager curiosity the transverse section
of the brain," for he can perceive "the number of parts,
their distinctions, connections, structure, uses." Similarly the painter, or anyone else who has become aware of
the harmonious diversity in any aspect of nature, dis-
covers it elsewhere. The painter, who has the ability to
represent "all [the] distinctions in nature" on canvas,
helps others become aware of them. ". . . by exciting
curiosity, and inviting a comparison between the object
and the representation, . . . imitation renders an object,
[perhaps] displeasing in itself, a source of pleasure, not
by repetition of the same idea, but by suggesting new
ideas, by detecting new proportions, and endless shades
of difference, just as a close and continued contemplation of the object itself would do." Thus art becomes
"the microscope of the mind," by accustoming the mind
to what Tucker had called "trains of imaginations" and
what Hazlitt calls "trains of feeling" which are recalled
not only by the objects represented in a work of art but
by "every object," so that we see it not as a "confused
mass" but as "a little universe in itself."[73] A work of art
duplicates patterns of general experience and therefore,
through association, becomes a symbol of universal or-

der. It is not, as Addison believed it might sometimes be, merely a means of approximating the "pleasing Shows and Apparitions" of nature.[74]

The "order" which Hazlitt prizes most in a poem, play, or novel seems to be an assemblage of traits in a character, a diversity of striking actions, and a relation between character and action, all of which the audience recognizes as true and natural.[75] Character and action, in turn, are rendered palpable by particulars that carry a charge of generally established associations. Hazlitt requires "translation" to be a far more general thing than Tucker defines it. Like Wordsworth, he would have a poet direct his attention to the "knowledge which all men carry about with them."[76] The poet's emotion-laden particulars must, in a great work of art, "express" the essential quality of a person or thing. ". . . expression is the great test and measure of a genius for painting, and the fine arts." Objects become expressive—as Tucker had explained—through "some precise association with pleasure or pain," but for Hazlitt expression is something more objectively symbolic than in Tucker because Hazlitt assumes a sympathetic poet or artist whose general associations are stimulated and directed by intense feeling. To define "truth of character" and then to reveal "the soul of nature," a poet or painter must have the emotional intensity that Hazlitt calls "gusto." "Michael Angelo's forms are full of gusto. . . . His limbs convey an idea of muscular strength, of moral grandeur, and even of intellectual dignity. . . ." Expression may depend on "moral" associations, as in Michael Angelo, or on synaesthetic ones. Titian's "flesh-colour . . . seems sensitive and alive all over; not merely to have the look and texture of flesh, but the feeling in itself. . . . In a word, gusto in painting is where the impression made on one sense *excites by affinity* those of another."[77]

"Chaucer's descriptions of natural scenery" show gusto
in their power to give "the very feeling of the air, the
coolness or moisture of the ground." Milton, who also
"has great gusto, . . . repeats his blows twice."

> Or where Chineses drive
> With sails and wind their *cany* waggons *light*.
>
> .   .   .   .   .   .
>
> Wild above rule or art, *enormous* bliss.[78]

The synaesthesia of *cany* and *light* is apparently matched,
in "moral expression," by the connotations of *enormous*.

Tucker had also found beauty in "succession" as long
as it did not—by becoming mere novelty—sacrifice the
ordering power of established associations. Succession
is "a variety of objects succeeding each other" or form-
ing a "multitude of assemblages." It pleases by "keeping up the play" of "sensation and reflection."[79] Hazlitt,
too, counts a good deal on a profusion of distinct parts
to provide aesthetic pleasure. One reason, he tells us,
why he likes a work of art to include a varied and siz-
able collection of objects and events is that this is the way
things are in "real life."[80] A work of art pleases by stim-
ulating customary trains of ideas and thus by suggesting
a familiar relationship among its parts, but it also pleases
because this process in itself gives the mind some enjoy-
able exercise. "The excitement of intellectual activity"
pleases, and pleases most of all by bringing the whole
mind into play. The merit of Hogarth's pictures lies in
their power "to fill up the void of the mind" with the
"number of ideas they excite."[81] Here Hazlitt is sharing
with a number of earlier writers the belief—derived
more or less from Longinus' *On the Sublime*—that the
contemplation of large objects or a large number of objects stretches the mind towards a pleasurable fulfillment
of its powers. Such objects or masses of objects were
called *great* or *sublime,* and their effects were frequently

distinguished from those of merely beautiful objects as being more intense and therefore more mind-filling. The eighteenth century, however, gave the mind a somewhat less active role than Longinus did, thinking more often of the passive enlargement of the spectator's mind than of the writer's elevation of soul and correlative loftiness of style.[82] The distinction between the sublime and the beautiful was so pervasive in the eighteenth century that Hazlitt's unstable use of these terms can hardly be traced to any specific source. His few references to Longinus do not convince us that he knew *On the Sublime* at first hand. We know, however, that he had read Burke and Reynolds on the subject and that he was well acquainted with the *Spectator*.

v

"Greatness," according to Addison, means not only "the Bulk of any single Object, but the Largeness of a whole View, considered as one entire Piece." It pleases because "our Imagination loves to be filled with an Object, or to grasp at anything too big for its Capacity." Since the mind hates restraint, it enjoys the freedom to "range abroad" through space and "lose it self" amidst a "Variety of Objects." Apparently this variety may be an aspect of greatness, but—as in "a Heaven adorned with Stars and Meteors"—it may also add the pleasures of novelty and beauty. Beauty resides in the opposite sex, in gay and varied colors, and in ordered variety. Except in the first category, it offers the imagination less intense pleasures than greatness does.[83] Although the efficient causes are different, the final cause of all the pleasures of the imagination is admiration for the "Goodness and Wisdom of the first Contriver." Created to enjoy the contemplation of his Creator, man naturally delights in whatever is "Great or Unlimited." He finds the Creator

equally generous in making the opposite sex attractive
and in dressing up the whole creation with pleasing colors and forms.[84] Like Addison, other writers frequently
identified the sublime with divine immensity or infinity,
but Burke attributes it to our concern for self-preservation. The source of the sublime is "whatever is fitted
. . . to excite the ideas of pain, and danger, that is to say,
whatever is in any sort terrible": fear, obscurity, power,
privation, vastness, infinity, succession and uniformity,
magnitude, difficulty, magnificence, powerful or flashing
lights, dark and gloomy colors, excessive or sudden or
uncertain sounds, angry cries of wild beasts, bitter smells
and tastes, and feelings of pain.[85] Such causes give us "an
idea of pain or danger," but when we know that we are
not actually imperiled, we experience the kind of "delight" which Burke calls sublime.[86] The sublime reaches
its "highest degree" in "astonishment," which fills the
mind and suspends "all its motions."[87] The less intense
and less mind-filling pleasures of beauty, on the other
hand, are ultimately caused by our enjoyment of "society"—that is, by our "sense of affection and tenderness"
toward other creatures. Anything—such as a small,
smooth, gradually varied, delicate, or mildly colored object—that induces this sense is therefore an efficient cause
of beauty.[88] Reynolds, on the other hand, does not separate the sublime from the beautiful. When he uses the
word *sublime,* it is to designate a superior kind of beauty
distinguished from the merely *elegant.* "The sublime
in Painting, as in Poetry, so overpowers, and takes such
possession of the whole mind, that no room is left for attention to minute criticism. The little elegancies of art
in the presence of these great ideas greatly expressed [by
Michael Angelo], lose all their value, and are, for the instant at least, felt to be unworthy of our notice."[89] Greatness of expression implies, evidently, not only "great and

general ideas" but great intensity of feeling that can
crowd out anything irrelevant. Reynolds' sublime is like
Burke's in this respect and in appearing "wild" and
"mysterious." It makes use of "sudden and bold projec-
tions" and abrupt angles, rather than gradual slopes and
"gentle inclination."[90]

Hazlitt does not systematically distinguish between
the sublime and the beautiful. The sublime may be
merely another name for beauty or, as in Reynolds, a
more exciting kind of beauty, which Hazlitt, like Reynolds, also calls "grandeur."[91] Nevertheless, Hazlitt occasionally attempts a distinction. Beauty *"harmonises"*;
the sublime *"aggrandises our impressions of things. . . .*
As sublimity is an excess of power, beauty is . . . the
blending and harmonising different powers or qualities
together, so as to produce a soft and pleasurable sensation."[92] Here we find, as in Burke, the contrast of power
and blended softness. In his essay "On Beauty" Hazlitt
makes a tripartite distinction much like Addison's. Here
he finds aesthetic pleasure in "custom, or the association
of ideas," in "novelty," and in the kind of beauty that
inheres in the object itself. The latter he describes in a
mixture of Addisonian and Burkeian terms as "a certain conformity of objects to themselves, a symmetry of
parts, a principle of proportion, gradation, and harmony." But it turns out that this kind of beauty is closer
to the kind described by Burke, who had denied "proportion" much of a share "in the formation of beauty."[93]
Gradation is the quality that Hazlitt emphasizes in his
illustrations, and in this essay beauty turns out to be
something smoothly gradual. A Greek face is beautiful
because "it is made up of lines corresponding with or
melting into each other"; in a head by Raphael "every
part . . . is blended together, and every sharp projection
moulded and softened down."[94] Hazlitt's admiration for

mellifluous verse also suggests this standard of beauty,[95] but in general his practical criticism and many theoretical statements show that, especially in poetry, he considers "aggrandising" by means of "the association of ideas" far more important than blending or than mere novelty. His favorite poetic form is the drama, and here he would agree with Ogilvie, who had called "a numerous and diversified series of incidents . . . sublime" and had added that it "forms . . . by far the most various and agreeable exercise" of the imagination.[96] As we have already noticed, even when Hazlitt is praising the novelty or originality of genius, his basis for aesthetic pleasure is the use of images with general associations.

When Hazlitt says that "grandeur is the principle of connexion between different parts,"[97] he is thinking, apparently, of linking by association. In Parts II and III of *The Sublime and Beautiful* association seems to account for the terror-producing powers of obscurity, privation, vastness, etc.; but in Part IV Burke explains that pain and fear arise, not from association, but directly from "an unnatural tension of the nerves" induced by various causes.[98] Hazlitt, as his objections to Hartley indicate, would hardly have followed Burke in ascribing these feelings to the mechanical effect of "the natural properties of things." Like Alison—although there is no evidence of direct influence—Hazlitt ascribes the sublime not to qualities in the object itself but, in Alison's terms, to its power "to awaken the imagination, and to lead it [by means of association] through every analogous idea that has place in the memory."[99] The creation or the appreciation of the sublime requires the unimpeded flow of ideas linked by strong feeling. Like Dr. Johnson, Hazlitt finds sublimity in the "aggregation" which "at once fills the whole mind"; but whereas Johnson means

that the great, general thought must not be sacrificed to
minutiae, Hazlitt means that the trains of association
must not be interrupted by irrelevant associations.
Imagination brings "the general forms and aggregate
masses of our ideas . . . into play" by "finding out something similar in things generally alike, or with like
feelings attached to them." Any incongruity "puts an
end to the sublime or beautiful."[100] Hazlitt does not
deny that "things thrown into masses" are especially exciting to the imagination,[101] but the aggregation that he
is mainly interested in takes place in the mind: both
the poet's and the reader's. This process unifies a variety
of images and, in addition, all the faculties and the will.
Hazlitt, who seems to have lost most of his interest in religion by the time he left Hackney College[102] and who
never regarded self-preservation as an adequate explanation for the higher operations of the mind, does not follow Addison or Burke in discovering a final cause for
sublime pleasure in either pious admiration or self-re-
garding passion. He is satisfied to trace this pleasure to
the discovery of truth and to the correlative realization
of one's own powers, mental and moral. Shakespeare's
characters extend these powers as "passion modified by
passion . . . call[s] into play all the resources of the understanding and all the energies of the will. . . . The human
soul is made the sport of fortune, the prey of adversity:
it is stretched on the wheel of destiny, in restless ecsta-
sy."[103] In impassioned or sublime poetry, a searching
complex of association completely involves the reader's
capacity for thought, feeling, and moral judgment. In
prizing this extended mental activity, Hazlitt is typically
eighteenth century; but in giving the mind an active
role therein he might be considered more Longinian
than, say, Addison. The difference can hardly be traced
to Hazlitt's knowledge of Longinus. It results, rather,

from the imagination having acquired, since Addison's time, new creative powers attributed to association in a state of intense feeling.

The imagination, as Hazlitt generally uses the term, may be defined as a faculty which, through perceiving similarities, combines concrete particulars with feelings to give immediate expression to universal truths. These truths are intuited by the poet or artist whose habitual sympathy with other people has made him aware of what is general and important in human experience or, more specifically, what is comprised in common patterns of association. The poet or artist must select and combine generally moving particulars to exploit these patterns and thus stimulate a complex of thought and feeling which adds up to "truth." The kind of aesthetic pleasure that interests Hazlitt most is that which comes from truth to nature: that is, from discovering some essential quality, sensory or abstract, in objects or characters; from recognizing order in a variety of objects and events, and from extending, in these processes, the powers of association. Through the number and variety of its emotionally charged and interrelated particulars, impassioned poetry touches off associations that probe the mind to its limits, bringing its moral and intellectual powers into harmonious fulfillment. This imaginative process is consummated in only the most impassioned poetry, which is tragedy.

IV

Tragedy

Tragic poetry . . . is the most impassioned
species . . . —"On Poetry in General" (1818).

THE ROMANTIC PERIOD, it has frequently been pointed
out, was unfavorable to the writing of tragedy because
its faith in progress achieved through reason or natural
goodness defined a non-tragic world.[1] To be sure, the
optimistic ideas of the Enlightenment, as well as the considerably less optimistic liberalism that marked the
opening decades of the nineteenth century, were inimical in certain respects to a tragic view of life. The theater itself, which offered sensational entertainment to
large and noisy audiences, also discouraged the writing
of tragedy and, for that matter, good plays of any kind.[2]
Yet this was a period in English literary history which, if
it did not produce great tragedies, produced great criticism of tragedy. Some critics, although subscribing to
natural-rights theory in various practical and theoretical
ways, nevertheless rejected its anti-tragic premises and
implications. A democratic position in practical politics
did not commit a writer to viewing human existence
solely within the historical framework of his political
ideas. Hazlitt and Keats are good examples of democrats
who, especially in their theories of morality and literature, turned away from some of the premises of Hobbes
and Locke. Because Hazlitt was both a political writer

and a literary critic, his writings are especially useful in tracing the line between natural-rights theory and Romanticism. For determining the powers of government Hazlitt accepted the rational world of liberal politics, but morally and aesthetically he rejected it, thereby defining one boundary of Romanticism and opening up a tragic view of life.

A world, like Hobbes', apprehended by the senses and ordered by reason, a world of efficient causes only, in which evil becomes merely unreasonable selfish behavior, avoidable by a more accurate calculation of consequences—this world, it is hardly necessary to point out, is not that of tragedy. Tragedy may assume a moral order, although sometimes one differing from man-made morality, but it is an order attributable to final causes and knowable, not by moral calculus, but by intensity of experience; an order, furthermore, that exalts man more by his defiance of consequences than by his calculation of them, and one whose rewards and punishments are not primarily material and physical. There have been, of course, political theorists—as well as countless people thinking and acting politically—who have extended natural-rights theory beyond the dimensions of sense and reason and thus made more room for a tragic view; while there have been others who bound the theory even more closely to physical rewards and selfish calculation. This stretching and narrowing of Hobbes' and Locke's two-dimensional world, we have noticed, is evident in Burke's *Reflections* and the ensuing controversy, in which natural-rights theory is most narrowly conceived by Malthus or, more accurately, by current applications of his principle of population, such as that in the *Quarterly* for 1817.[3]

If Malthus' followers like the writer in the *Quarterly* are guilty of optimism, it is a very sober kind. In their

widely accepted view, which had cramped natural-rights
theory down to freedom to buy and sell (and, in practice, denied even this freedom to all but the ruling class),
the thing that is adverse to tragedy is not the optimism
but those premises that tended to confine human aspira-
tion to selfish calculation and rational goals. It is true
that these premises had once encouraged an easy optimism and would do so again;[4] but here the important
difference between the *Quarterly*'s view and Hazlitt's is
not in the expectation of improvement but in Hazlitt's
conception of the human mind as creative and free; or,
in other words, in his emphasis on imagination as the
faculty that determines truth and morality.

i

Since poetic truth is directly proportional to passion,
it follows that the truest poetry is "the most impassioned
species"; and this species, says Hazlitt, is tragedy.[5] Tragedy could be written, in fact, only in an age when passions flourished with elemental intensity.[6] Comedy, on
the other hand, necessarily limits the emotions of the
writer and the audience because it restricts sympathetic
identification with character. Both tragedy and comedy,
according to Hazlitt, depend on "the difference between
what things are, and what they ought to be." In the expected or customary or proper course of events B should
follow A; but C turns up instead. Depending on the degree of interest one has in the occurrence of B, the sub-
stitution of C will be tragic or comic. The tragic
damatist "heightens" the interest in B (the hero's triumph, perhaps) so that the audience's sympathy is
stronger than its self-love and the occurrence of C (the
hero's death) is lamentable. On the other hand, the comic dramatist "loosens" the interest in B (a hypocrite's
getting away with his fraud) so that the audience's "self-

love is stronger than [its] sympathy" and the occurrence
of C (the hypocrite's exposure) is amusing.[7]

Too active an imagination, therefore, may be a handicap to a comic writer. Hazlitt "cannot help thinking
. . . that Molière was as great, or a greater comic genius
than Shakspeare," for in Shakespeare's comedies "the
spirit of humanity and the fancy of the poet greatly pre-
vail over the mere wit and satire, [so] that we sympathise
with his characters oftener that we laugh at them."
Shakespeare and Ben Jonson lived in the "comparatively rude age" of the "comedy of nature," when society
did not offer a model for what both Hazlitt and Lamb
call "artificial comedy." Man's natural weaknesses may
be laughable, but it is only in "a highly advanced state of
civilisation" where he apes "the extravagances of other
men" that man becomes truly ridiculous.[8] Thus the ar-
tificiality of Restoration comedy is a matter, not of inaccurate representation, but of the age represented; in fact,
the excellence of Restoration comedy lies in its being an
accurate, although comparatively unemotional, representation of a certain kind of society. Here and elsewhere in Hazlitt's criticism, the word "artificial" implies
indifference or self-love as distinct from "natural"
sympathy.[9]

Although he limits its role, Hazlitt does not deny
imagination a place in comedy. Given his definition of
imagination as part of perception, he cannot exclude it;
but comedy also requires some *heightening* of the imagination. Comparing the comedies of Shakespeare and
Ben Jonson, Hazlitt objects that there is too little freedom in the latter's imitation of nature.[10] Nor does Hazlitt deny the truth and morality of comedy. In relation
to its time, Restoration comedy was moral in its representation of truth and consequent correction of vice; and
in relation to a later time ("from which the same sort of

affectation and pretence are banished by a greater knowledge of the world, or by their successful exposure on the
stage")[11] artificial comedy, because it attains the "truth"
and "decency" of internal consistency and obedience to
its own laws, is still not morally offensive.[12]

Hazlitt does not say that comedy lacks values dependent on imagination. But comedy takes a less sympathetic
—and therefore less revealing—view of human nature,
and to the extent that it reduces the element of identification, it is less true and less moral than tragedy. Hazlitt
might have written, as Arnold did write, "Tragedy
breasts the pressure of life. Comedy eludes it, half liber-
ates itself from it by irony."[13]

The epic, too, although not requiring the kind of detachment necessary to comedy, requires another kind
that limits its scope. Hazlitt places Milton among the
four great English poets of the imagination[14] but nevertheless inferior to Shakespeare. Milton had "a mighty
intellect" and great imaginative power; "the fervour of
his imagination melts down and renders malleable, as in
a furnace, the most contradictory materials" and extends
its power to "musical expression" that makes his "blank
verse . . . the only blank verse in the language (except
Shakspeare's) that deserves the name of verse."[15] But his
excellence is achieved in a form inferior to the dramatic.
"In general, the interest in Milton is essentially epic, and
not dramatic; and the difference between the epic and
the dramatic is this, that in the former the imagination
produces the passion, and in the latter the passion produces the imagination. The interest of epic poetry arises
from the contemplation of certain objects in themselves
grand and beautiful: the interest of dramatic poetry
from sympathy with the passions and pursuits of others.
. . ."[16] The epic is to tragedy as "contemplation" is to
"sympathy," or as "terror and pity" are to "admiration

and delight." "The objects of dramatic poetry . . . take us by surprise, or force us upon action . . ."; whereas those of "epic poetry affect us . . . by magnitude and distance, by their permanence and universality."[17] *Paradise Lost* shows the effects of something less than an intense degree of sympathy. In Milton the intensity of sympathetic feeling has not burned out the purely personal as it has in Shakespeare; the "bias and opinions of the man" remain "in the creations of the poet." Milton, unlike Shakespeare, did not "mingle with the crowd" but "lived apart, . . . carefully excluding from his mind whatever might distract its purposes."[18] His characters are likewise remote from actuality. They lack the fluid variety—the "continual composition and decomposition of . . . elements"—found in Shakespeare's characters. Adam and Eve "convey to us the ideas of sculpture"; Satan represents "the abstract love of power, of pride, of self-will personified."[19] Although, as Hazlitt grants, Homer's characters are not merely abstractions, the epic remains, for Hazlitt, less interesting, less varied, less intense, less excellent than the dramatic.

ii

Hazlitt's definition of impassioned poetry implies, of course, the morality of tragedy. "The stage . . . is the best teacher of morals, for it is the truest and most intelligible picture of life"—and tragedy offers the truest picture of all. Since an unselfish concern for others becomes more acute through habit, both the writing and the reading (or witnessing) of tragedy are moral experiences. Hazlitt defies "any great tragic writer to despise that nature which he understands, or that heart which he has probed, with all its rich bleeding materials of joy and sorrow."[20] The audience's experience is equally moral. Tragedy identifies the audience with the tragic character and thus with humanity in general. What one is purged of, says Hazlitt, is not pity and fear but selfishness, which is replaced by pity and fear for others.[21] The evil displayed in impassioned tragedy contributes to pleasure, but it is a moral pleasure. In the tragedies of Edward Moore and Lillo—poetry of sensibility—evil lies "like a dead weight upon the mind"; but in the tragedies of Shakespeare evil falls into true perspective among the "rich depths of the human soul" that the poet has revealed.[22] So displayed, and thus accompanied by deep human sympathy, evil excites "our sense and desire of the opposite good." Catharsis is not simply escape from selfish isolation, for "our sympathy with actual suffering is lost in the strong impulse given to our natural affections, and carried away with the swelling tide of passion, that gushes from and relieves the heart."[23]

But the representation of evil gives pleasure in still another way, for it appeals to "the common love of strong excitement."[24] Hazlitt's doctrine of sympathetic identification leads him to emphasize pity, but the tragic must have the "means of exciting terror"[25] as well. The tragic writer must not allow any philosophical system or any other premeditated conclusions to exclude "awe" and "mystery," "vastness and obscurity," "sharp calamities," or "the dark and doubtful views of things"[26]—not only because they are parts of life that the poet must assimilate to his art but because they stimulate emotion and therefore imaginative activity. Hazlitt's fondness for vastness and obscurity, awe and terror, recalls Burke once more. Burke and Hazlitt agree that tragedy is the most impassioned kind of poetry; that we delight in the misfortunes and pains of others; that we enjoy expressing every passion we are capable of, no matter what sort; that pity for the victims of an evil makes us seek the opposite good; and that an audience would get up and leave a tragedy in order to see a hanging.[27] But there is also an important difference between Burke and Hazlitt. Burke says, "In imitated distresses the only difference is the pleasure resulting from the effects of imitation; for it is never so perfect, but we can perceive it is an imitation, and on the principle are somewhat pleased with it."[28] But for Hazlitt a tragedy does more than add the pleasure of seeing a correspondence between the imitation and the thing imitated. The pleasure of tragedy defines a human being confronting evil. This pleasure harmonizes sense, feeling, and intellect. "Impassioned poetry is an emanation of the moral and intellectual part of our nature, as well as of the sensitive—of the desire to know, the will to act, and the power to feel. . . ." We have the power to *feel* (to hate as well as to love), and we enjoy the exercise of that power, whether we are watching a tragedy or a hanging. But we also enjoy the power of *knowing* the thing we hate; and in poetry the object of our feeling is defined exactly, so that our feeling is refined by the precise knowledge of its appropriateness. At the same time, when this object of our feeling is represented accurately and we feel both the justness of the representation and of our feeling toward it, we are impelled to *act* accordingly. The tragic experience, therefore, is a matter of self-knowledge and self-realization (emotionally, intellectually, and morally) in the face of evil. It offers freedom, not from the consequences of evil—which are inescapable—but from being deceived by it.[29]

Hazlitt arrived at this definition of tragic experience by rejecting the limited world of Hobbes and Locke, Godwin and Malthus. He rejected it as excluding parts of human life that the poet must assimilate and as excluding, in addition, those faculties necessary for that assimilation. Thus he rejected some premises of natural-

rights theory that work against the tragic view: the physical basis of morality, the exclusion of final causes, the
basic rationalism of human beings, the reasoned identification of interests, the confusion of moral with material
progress, and the conception of evil as something that
reason can comprehend and therefore avoid. But he
continued to champion the natural rights of liberty and
equality—along with fraternity (achieved through sympathetic identification) as necessary to the realization of
these rights. Tragedy, like democracy, requires the selflessness of self-fulfillment.

There is, of course, a paradox in Hazlitt's insistence
on the selflessness of tragic experience. The reader (or
the auditor) becomes humanity, but humanity also becomes the reader and the tragic experience a piece of gigantic egotism. In tragedy, too, there is a point where
sympathy stops and self-love begins, but it is not the
same point as in comedy. Lionel Trilling, in objecting
to Arnold's estimate of comic irony, says that "irony is as
much the adjunct of tragedy as of comedy,"[30] yet I think
that a distinction should be emphasized. The irony of
comedy requires detachment from character and sympathy with a social norm, while the irony of tragedy requires sympathy with character and detachment from a
first cause. The Promethean egotism of tragedy is gener-
ic, not individual; it unites humanity against a morally
inferior (or at least morally different) universe.

But Hazlitt's moral emphasis does tend to obscure or
confuse the element of tragic irony. In tragedy immutable law brings disaster to characters whom men would
judge good, or mainly good, as well as to those who are
evil. We pity a character who, although mainly admirable, is destroyed because of a relatively minor fault—or
perhaps for no fault at all. As his doom approaches, we
feel fear, not only for the tragic character, but for our-

selves. Both pity and fear are intensified if the character possesses excellence of some sort. The inappropriateness of the character's fate, with respect to his excellence, gives rise to tragic irony.

The moralistic critic may, with Samuel Johnson, prefer a "just distribution of good or evil";[31] or he may be tempted to find some moral appropriateness in the tragic outcome. This is a temptation that Hazlitt does not altogether resist. He scorns, it is true, the "professed moralist in literature" and the crude poetic justice of plays like *The London Merchant*;[32] but to his explanation of catharsis Hazlitt adds that tragedy "corrects [the] fatal excesses [of the passions] in ourselves by pointing to the greater extent of sufferings and of crimes to which they have led others."[33] Elsewhere Hazlitt is more guarded in explaining the evil in tragedy. In Greek tragedy, he says, the discipline of a higher power is clear and inflexible because Greek "religion or mythology . . . was material and definite"; whereas in Christian religion or mythology "we can find only unlimited, undefined power . . . [and] belief [in] an universal, invisible principle of all things, a vastness and obscurity which confounds our perceptions, while it exalts our piety."[34] Perhaps, although it would suggest an interest rather unusual for Hazlitt, this means that an enlightened audience should recognize in tragic misfortune the working of a benevolent, if obscure, principle. But what Hazlitt is mainly interested in—what he finds *natural* or *truthful*—is the behavior of characters under "given circumstances," whether these are the circumstances of Greek or of Christian mythology. Hazlitt is not really concerned with the relative truth of Greek and Christian mythologies as ideas external to the plays. Both mythologies are true in that they have become part of human experience as realized by tragic poets. If Hazlitt prefers, in tragedy, what he calls the Christian mythology, it is only because this belief allows the imagination more freedom. Greek tragedy, although "natural," confines its imitation more strictly to "the external object," whereas English tragedy of the ages of Elizabeth and James "seeks to identify the original impression with whatever else, within the range of thought or feeling, can strengthen, relieve, adorn or elevate it."[35] This is the difference between "a Grecian temple" and "the ruins of a Gothic castle." The former "is beautiful in itself, and excites immediate admiration." The latter "have no beauty or symmetry to attract the eye; and yet they excite a more powerful and romantic interest from the ideas with which they are habitually associated."[36] If English tragedy is truer than Greek tragedy, it is because the poet's imagination has ranged farther and not because the poet has postulated a benevolent deity.

iii

Despite his hints that tragedy illustrates poetic justice, Hazlitt's practical criticism as well as his theory emphasizes the morality of compassion. The tragedy of poetic justice, like comedy, requires detachment; for the moral to take effect, the audience or reader must at some point detach himself morally from the victim and his fate. But Hazlitt would keep detachment from character at a minimum; he implies greater detachment from a first cause, of which, we have seen, he grants the "obscurity." In the *Characters of Shakespear's Plays* (1817) —that is, in Hazlitt's own version of Shakespeare's mythology—the tragic character's fate remains inappropriate to his excellent qualities. Hazlitt wrote the *Characters of Shakespear's Plays,* he tells us, "to illustrate by a reference to each play" Pope's observation that Shakespeare's characters are "nature herself."[37] The book has

the faults that its purpose suggests and some others be-
sides. Hazlitt tends to lift Shakespeare's characters out
of the plays and treat them as though they were actual
acquaintances not under the laws of any particular work
of art; the analytical passages are perceptive but too few
and too soon broken off; and the texture of both thought
and feeling sometimes slackens in a series of long quotations. Nevertheless, especially when his admiration is
strongest, Hazlitt recreates many of Shakespeare's characters with sharp and telling insight.

Hazlitt is constantly concerned with the likeness of
Shakespeare's characters to real people. For Aristotle
the tragic character, although imperfect, is *morally* superior to "the men of the present day";[38] but until recent times tragic characters have usually been superior
in rank and power as well. Hazlitt was not one to like
tyranny in a play or anywhere else, although he grants
that "wrong dressed out in pride, pomp, and circumstance, has more attraction [for the imagination] than
abstract right."[39] While analyzing Shakespeare's characters, Hazlitt is more interested in identifying the tragic
character with "men of the present day" than in any sort
of differentiation. "It is *we* who are Hamlet. . . . Hamlet
is as little of the hero as a man can well be. . . ." "We
feel neither respect nor love for the deposed [Richard].
. . . He is, however, human in his distresses; for to feel
pain, and sorrow, weakness, disappointment, remorse
and anguish, is the lot of humanity, and we sympathize
with him accordingly. The sufferings of the man make
us forget that he ever was a king."[40] No one will insist
that kingship is necessary to human excellence; but Hazlitt, who grants that "the subject [of tragedy] may not be
a source of much triumph" and calls Lear "a poor crazy
old man, who has nothing sublime about him but his
afflictions,"[41] may seem to make room for the merely

pathetic character who is appealing only in his distress
or affliction. Nevertheless, it is Greek tragedy and Elizabethan and Jacobean tragedy that Hazlitt puts in the
top rank, unchallenged as tragedies of *nature*.[42] If Hazlitt tends to bring the characters down to the level of
ordinary human beings, they are still involved in terrible and awesome events and usually display "that mental
fortitude and heroic cast of thought which alone makes
tragedy endurable—that renders its sufferings pathetic,
or its struggles sublime."[43] The mind of Lear "is like a
tall ship driven about by the winds, buffeted by the furi-
ous waves, but that still rides above the storm, having
its anchor fixed in the bottom of the sea; or it is like the
sharp rock circled by the eddying whirlpool that foams
and beats against it, or like the solid promontory pushed
from its basis by the force of an earthquake."[44] Herein
lies the excellence of the *Characters of Shakespear's
Plays*: not in defining the overall pattern of tragedy but
in making vivid the existence of human beings as they
confront terrible situations.[45] Hazlitt's idea of human
greatness is democratic but not sentimental; if it occasionally fails to realize the possibilities of tragic irony, it
also widens the range of tragic effect. Hazlitt does not
doubt that all human beings, apart from any distinctions
of rank and power, may deserve the intense sympathy of
poet and audience.

Since Hazlitt's time, the dispossessing of tragic heroes
has continued, so that today, more often than not, the
tragic hero has been stripped politically, economically,
and even spiritually. The last century has shrunk man
in relation to the physical universe and minimized his
free agency. Although, in twentieth-century tragedies,
some heroes remain great in their dispossession, many
have become only pathetic. Hazlitt represents a point

along the way, where the idea of tragic greatness has been generalized but not seriously diluted.

Tragedy has generally been considered a greater literary achievement than comedy. Aristotle, with his emphasis on seriousness, purgation, and characters better than actual people, has lent authority to this preference, although he does not clearly award tragedy the higher place. More explicit in their choice of tragedy over comedy are Sidney, Milton, Addison, A. W. Schlegel, and Arnold. A modern critic, Joseph Wood Krutch, has called tragedy "the greatest and the most difficult of the arts"; and a modern mathematician and philosopher, Bertrand Russell, has called it "of all the arts . . . the proudest, the most triumphant."[46] A good deal of testimony, therefore, supports Hazlitt's preference for tragedy.

Hazlitt explains this preference by the degree of sympathetic identification that tragedy requires of the poet and arouses in the reader. Hence tragedy's truth and morality. Hazlitt's own identification with character accounts for both the weakness and the strength of his criticism of tragedy. The principal weakness is his over-identification with character, which tends to confuse art with life and to isolate character from structure. On the other hand, sympathetic identification has provided Hazlitt with a firmer basis than poetic justice for judging the morality of great tragedies; and almost always his process of identifying the reader with a tragic character, like the good performance of a good tragedy, intensifies the reader's feeling of human dignity and the irony of human fate. Hazlitt's case for the superiority of tragedy must be supported by his practical criticism—the work of his own imagination.

V

Fancy and Wit

> Young, . . . Gray, or Akenside, only follow in
> the train of Milton and Shakspeare: Pope and
> Dryden walk by their side, though of unequal
> stature, and are entitled to a first place in the
> lists of fame.—"On Dryden and Pope" (1818).

SINCE IT TAKES a "comparatively barbarous" society for
the poetry of imagination to flourish, Hazlitt found English poetry declining through "successive gradations"
since "the time of Elizabeth." It fell off, first, to "the
poetry of fancy . . . in the time of Charles I.; and again
from the poetry of fancy to that of wit, as in the reign of
Charles II. and Queen Anne. It degenerated into the
poetry of mere common places, both in style and
thought, in the succeeding reigns: as in the latter part of
the last century, it was transformed, by means of the
French Revolution, into the poetry of paradox."[1] Each
of these inferior kinds of poetry lacks the truth of great
poetry; for each kind, in one way or another, limits the
range or depth of feeling. In relation to the imaginative
process and its consummation, poetry that is fanciful,
"common place," or paradoxical simply has the qualities
of great poetry to a lesser degree; but the poetry of wit
has a "kind and degree of excellence" of its own.[2]

Something apart from "truth to nature," therefore,
must account for this excellence. Hazlitt is almost always concerned with the methods whereby a poem may

represent nature, and this emphasis obscures his recognition of any kind or order of truth peculiar to a work of art.[3] Hazlitt's imitation of nature, to be sure, calls for heightened realism, in which essential qualities are defined by emotion-charged images. But, Hazlitt seems to say, poetry is never more successful than when it duplicates experience with nature. The "poetry of nature" exerts "the same power over the minds of [its] readers, that nature does." It is "a copy of the indestructible forms and everlasting impulses of nature, welling out from the bosom . . . or stamped upon the senses. . . ."[4] As something with its own laws and order, however, poetry is more closely distinguished from nature when Hazlitt analyzes and evaluates the poetry of wit.

i

The structure of fancy is less clearly distinguished. Hazlitt does not define *fancy* as explicitly as he does *imagination, wit, common places,* or *paradox.* Hazlitt—unlike Coleridge and such eighteenth-century writers as William Duff and Dugald Stewart[5]—does not often distinguish fancy as less creatively plastic, less serious and true, than imagination. Hazlitt's historical scale seems to limit the poetry of fancy to a definite period and to a relatively slight decline from imaginative excellence. In his criticism of individual works, however, *fancy* (even when it can be distinguished from *imagination*) suggests a much wider range of meaning. Hazlitt does not, by any means, confine the poetry of fancy to the reign of Charles I. It seems to begin with Beaumont and Fletcher—"the first writers who . . . departed from the genuine tragic style of the age of Shakespear"[6]—and to continue into Hazlitt's own time with Campbell, Moore, and even —in *Endymion*—Keats.[7] The effects of fancy are equally

diverse. The play of fancy does not remove Spenser
from the ranks of the imaginative poets, but for Thomas
Moore it is disastrous.[8]

When Hazlitt makes a distinction between *fancy* and
imagination, the former occurs in contexts which disso-
ciate it from passion and therefore from such imaginative qualities as objective truth, built-in judgment,
seriousness, sublimity, and unity. Often fancy appears
linked with wit (the faculty that "disconnects our sympathy from passion and power"): "The Rape of the
Lock is a double-refined essence of wit and fancy. . . ."[9]
Furthermore, in the tradition of Hobbes, fancy sometimes implies subjective fantasy: "Swift . . . endeavoured to escape from the persecution of realities into the
regions of fancy. . . ."[10] The term also suggests irrespon-
sibility and triviality. Fancy is "sportive," "exuberant,"
"truant"; it is "richness running riot"; it "pirouettes"
and "flutters in the gale."[11] It is a quality of the "effeminate" poetry of mere sensation without moral or structural sinew. It fails to aggregate the parts of a poem into
a sublime massiveness. It falls short of integrity not only
among the images themselves but also in character and
action. *Endymion,* a fanciful poem, lacks the firm interplay of character and action that only imagination can
consummate; it is all "soft and fleshy, without bone or
muscle."[12] This depreciation of fancy because it is "trivial," "truant," "sportive," "playful," and "rambling"
rather than "solemn," "true," "sublime," "consistent,"
and "regular," or because it deals with "the material
world" and escapes from "intellectual and moral subjects" to "appearances with which our senses are conversant" was not uncommon in and before Hazlitt's
time.[13] Fancy, obviously, had retained a number of less
admirable qualities that Dr. Johnson and others attributed to the imagination.

Since Hazlitt is so hard on fanciful poets, it may
seem odd that, on his scale of poetic excellence, he
places the poetry of fancy second only to the poetry of
the imagination. But this would not be the only instance of his assigning individual poets higher or lower
rank than that suggested by the historical category in
which he placed them. Although chronologically
Wordsworth must be classified as a poet of paradox, at
the bottom of Hazlitt's scale, Hazlitt ranks him almost
among Chaucer, Spenser, Shakespeare, and Milton.[14]
Hazlitt was sufficiently devoted to his historical explanation of declining excellence[15] to refer to it frequently,
but he was also a good enough critic not to let it overrule
his judgment of individual authors and works. Regarding the poetry of fancy, however, there is a second
reason for the apparent discrepancy between Hazlitt's
practical criticism and his historical theory.[16] Hazlitt's
definition of fancy is very unstable; it may designate not
only a kind of middle ground distinct from both imagination and wit but, probably more often, the creative or
combining faculty that includes imagination and does
not always exclude wit. Its effects may be serious or comic, tender or caustic, true or false.[17] Whether or not
Hazlitt admires it almost always depends on its combination with other qualities. Like Coleridge he admits fancy into a poem as harmonious "drapery" provided the
poem also includes truly imaginative coalescence.[18] In
Spenser, a poet of the imagination, fancy is admirable;
still linked closely with tragic passion, it does not keep
Beaumont and Fletcher from a place just outside "the
age of Shakespear"; but in Campbell and Moore it has
further declined into the egocentricity of the poets of
paradox. Combined in metaphysical poetry with "ingenuity of thought," fancy partakes both of wit and, sometimes, of the warmer qualities of imagination.[19] Hazlitt

is fond of those witty and fanciful poets—like Suckling, Waller, and Marvell—whose fancy is "light and pleasing," "lively, tender, and elegant," or "gay" and "good humoured," rather than "keen and caustic" or "rigid" and "harsh" as in Rochester and Donne.[20]

ii

Hazlitt's treatment of wit is more precise and, for purposes of analysis, much more satisfactory. *Wit*, like *fancy* and *imagination*, had many meanings in the seventeenth and eighteenth centuries. Hobbes uses *wit*, or *good wit*, to comprise all *"virtues intellectual,"* both natural and acquired, such as judgment, prudence, reason, fancy, and purposeful imagining. But he also narrows the meaning of *wit* to equate it with *fancy* alone, the unreliable faculty of seeing similitudes.[21] It is wit in this sense, of course, that Locke depreciates, along with fancy, as a "perfect cheat."[22] But *wit* had other meanings that kept the word from completely sharing the degeneration suffered by *fancy*. In Dryden and Pope wit sometimes comes close to meaning poetry itself or at least the language of poetry properly adapted to the subject.[23] The idea of wit as a comparing faculty persists in Dr. Johnson, who describes wit as "at once natural and new, that which, though not obvious, is, upon its first production, acknowledged to be just." Insofar as wit's effect on the reader is concerned, this is not unlike Romantic definitions of the imagination; but also, in a "more rigorous and philosophical" definition which includes the wit of the metaphysical poet, Johnson defines wit "as a kind of *discordia concors;* a combination of dissimilar images, or discovery of occult resemblances in things apparently unlike."[24] Addison's definition suggests both of Johnson's: wit "consists in . . . a Resemblance and Congruity of Ideas" which "gives *Delight* and *Surprize* to the Reader. . . . The Ideas should not lie too near one another in the Nature of things; for where the Likeness is obvious, it gives no Surprize."[25]

Hazlitt's definition of wit is much like Johnson's second definition, but with more attention paid to the effects of dissimilarity. "Wit or ludicrous invention" is "the eloquence of indifference," which uses "accidental or nominal resemblances" to "disconnect our sympathy from passion and power. . . ." To illustrate a witty comparison he cites the familiar lobster couplet from *Hudibras:*

> And, like a lobster boil'd, the morn
> From black to red, began to turn. . . .[26]

The redness shared by the morn and the lobster is "accidental" rather than "natural," for the two have little else in common. In fact, the evident differences between the morn and the lobster are essential to the couplet's effect. In this case the lobster even had to be cooked, and the reader presumably is filled with self-loving appetite or, for that matter, aversion. With its impertinent suggestions, therefore, the comparison "disconnects" the reader's admiration from poetic descriptions of the sunrise. Sympathy may also be disconnected, Hazlitt adds, for "a mere dry observation on human life, without elevation or enthusiasm," as in Pope's lines:

> 'Tis with our judgments as our watches, none
> Go just alike; yet each believes his own. . . .[27]

Both the cooked lobster and the watch fall in Hazlitt's category of the "artificial" objects which are appropriate materials for wit. The poet of imagination avoids such objects in favor of those "natural" or value-charged images that weave a powerful texture of association and feeling. To the poet who would find materials

significant and moving to a large number of readers,
"natural objects" are useful because of our "habitual attachments" to them; whereas "works of art" (by which
Hazlitt means, in this instance, man-made objects) want
"habitual and universal interest."[28] Wordsworth and
Coleridge, of course, make a similar distinction.[29] Unless artificial materials become poetical through "habitual attachment," Hazlitt continues, they suggest only
individual and practical concerns, satisfying self-love
and thus blocking up "the avenues to the imagination
and the heart."[30] Emotionally charged images, super-
charged by their proximity to each other, are necessary
to evoke the complex of associations and sympathy that
the "truest" poetry must comprise. Characters, too, may
restrict a poem's truth if they are drawn from an "artificial" society rather than a "natural" one uncorrupted
by the advance of civilization. Just as tragedy, in which
the characters are highly sympathetic, is truer than comedy, so is Shakespeare's comedy of nature, in which the
characters are only *naturally* foolish, truer than Restoration comedy, in which the characters are *artificially*
foolish.[31]

The poetry of wit—like comedy and for the same reason—is excluded from the first rank of greatness, since it
requires the "disconnection of sympathy." Yet, with
Pope and Dryden, the poetry of wit attains a high rank.
Pope did not, like the "poet of nature," feel things "in
their universal interest" but "preferred the artificial . . .
in external objects" and "in passion" as well. But these
materials are appropriate to his "chief excellence,"
which lies more in "checking" than in "encouraging"
passion—in "diminishing" the elevated or, conversely,
in "adorning the trivial." Pope shows us the world
through the wrong end of a microscope, "where things
are seen in their minutest circumstances and slightest

shades of difference; where the little becomes gigantic, the deformed beautiful, and the beautiful deformed." Yet, within this inverted world, Pope's accomplishment is so "exquisite" that, along with Dryden, he is second only to the greatest poets. Young, Gray, and Akenside "follow in the train of Milton and Shakspeare," but "Pope and Dryden walk by their side, though of an unequal stature, and are entitled to a first place in the lists of fame."[32] Apparently Pope and Dryden surpass Young, Gray, and Akenside not in greater truth to nature, but in putting their lightly charged materials to better use.

One wishes that Hazlitt had analyzed in more detail the "exquisiteness" of at least one of Pope's poems; but even so he clearly recognizes a "unity of impression" derived from the nice adjustment of disparate images to each other and to the effect of the poem as a whole, and admires a kind of internal order achieved even at the expense of "natural" links among the images. The tensions which hold the images together depend as much on diverting as on reviving the usual flow of associations. Wit is "imagination or fancy" inverted, whereby "evanescent and glancing impressions" which have little to do with "the nature of things" are combined for "surprise or contrast." The result is a world of "seeming analogy" and "mock-identity"[33] with its own laws and congruities.

Hazlitt also admires the poetry of wit because it is objective. He anticipates some more recent critics in disliking the "obsession with one's own emotions"[34] found in nineteenth-century poetry. Whereas the greatest poets objectify their material through sympathetic identification and the resulting intuition of universal truth, the poet of wit gains objectivity by "indifference" and detachment. The mock-heroic method in *The Beggar's Opera,* for instance, enables Gay to avoid some of Words-

worth's difficulties with low characters. In this work
"the scenes, characters, and incidents are, in themselves,
of the lowest and most disgusting kind"; but the characters' "sentiments and reflections" are those of "fine gen-
tlemen and ladies, satirists and philosophers."[35] When
Wordsworth "makes pedlars and ploughmen his heroes
and the interpreters of his sentiments," Hazlitt is ready
to "take leave" of such "low company";[36] but Gay has
made a similar "transformation without once violating
probability."[37] In Wordsworth "an intense intellectual
egotism swallows up every thing"; all the characters
are the poet.[38] But by assuming "the licence of the
mock-heroic style," Gay has done *"justice to nature."*
Thoughts and feelings which, if ascribed realistically to
low characters, would be false and sentimental become
probable within the mock-heroic framework and at the
same time bring out "with great felicity . . . the good
qualities and interesting emotions almost inseparable
from the lowest conditions." Furthermore, the mock-
heroic method makes the crimes of the low characters a
satire on the immoralities of the upper class.[39] Paradoxically Gay has used the method of wit—here the juxta-
position of low characters and fine manners: a scheme
both unrealistic and emotionally restricted—not only for
satire but to do "justice to nature." Polarities not only
attract but may also repel, and in either case, as Hazlitt
realizes, set up forces that are useful in getting a poem
off the ground of personal experience.

iii

There remains, of course, some reason for Wellek's
assertion that "on the whole, Hazlitt's attitude toward
witty and conceited poetry is quite negative."[40] Along
with Dr. Johnson, Hazlitt finds that the metaphysical

poets with their "far-fetched" comparisons "spoiled nature by art," applying to "serious subjects that quaint
and partial style of allusion which fits only what is light
and ludicrous"; whereas "the object of the poetry of
imagination is to raise or adorn one idea by another
more striking or more beautiful."[41] Cowley's description of Light is "too remote and degrading for serious
poetry, and yet is meant for such":

> First-born of Chaos, who so fair didst come
> From the old negro's darksome womb!

It is not difficult to agree with Hazlitt that this is "neither wit nor poetry."[42] Nevertheless, when Hazlitt insists
that "the slightest want of unity of impression destroys
the sublime; [and that] the detection of the smallest incongruity is an infallible ground to rest the ludicrous
upon,"[43] he seems to overlook some of the effects that incongruity may contribute to. He might also be taxed
with setting up an impossibly difficult standard, for a
comparison without "the smallest incongruity" would
be hard to find. In "On Shakspeare and Milton" Hazlitt
quotes, among other examples of imagination, from
Troilus and Cressida (III. iii. 222-225):

> Rouse yourself; and the weak wanton Cupid
> Shall from your neck unloose his amorous fold,
> And like a dew-drop from a lion's mane
> Be shook to air.

"Dew-drop" is probably a "natural" image variously appropriate to "weak wanton Cupid," but, if one persists,
incongruities and purely "selfish" interests may be
found in the same comparison.[44]

However, although he doubts that amorous planets
and wreathed souls of hair can bring a reader to serious
attention, Hazlitt is aware that a degree of incongruity
(if the word may include "remoteness," "surprise," and

"novelty") can sharpen, refine, or even intensify feeling. "From the remoteness of [Shakespeare's] combinations, and the celerity with which they are effected, they coalesce the more indissolubly together. The more the thoughts are strangers to each other, and the longer they have been kept asunder, the more intimate does their union seem to become. Their felicity is equal to their force. Their likeness is made more dazzling by their novelty. They startle, and take the fancy prisoner in the same instant."[45] Here Hazlitt somes close to a distinction made by Coleridge: "It is not always easy to distinguish between wit and fancy. When the whole pleasure received is derived from surprise at an unexpected turn of expression, then I call it wit; but when the pleasure is produced not only by surprise, but also by an image which remains with us and gratifies for its own sake, then I call it fancy."[46] Hazlitt, however, is explaining the effect of Shakespeare's *imagination* and is not using the word *fancy* to suggest a different or inferior faculty. This is not, of course, quite the effect of wit: here the awareness of difference is initial, not final. It is important in creating the final effect but is not part of that effect. Shakespeare's images are still "the most alike," although "placed at the greatest distance from each other." It is their "circumstances" that are dissimilar. In Dr. Johnson's words, these images, though "new," are still "natural."[47] Cupid is to be shaken like a dewdrop from a lion's mane, a blush is like a cold morning confronting the sun, applause is like a reverberating arch.[48] These images all have poetical associations; none is a manufactured product except the arch, and arches had long since been charged with appropriate feeling.

It is wit, however, that Hazlitt is concerned with in his analysis of *Lear*. The incongruity is sustained within a long sequence of "combinations," although again the

final effect is coalescence. Hazlitt recognizes the power
that wit may lend even to tragic poetry.

> Lear and the Fool are the sublimest instance I know of passion
> and wit united, or of imagination unfolding the most tremendous
> sufferings, and of burlesque on passion playing with it, aiding and
> relieving its intensity by the most pointed, but familiar and indif-
> ferent illustrations of the same thing in different objects, and on a
> meaner scale. The Fool's reproaching Lear with "making his
> daughters his mothers," his snatches of proverbs and old ballads,
> "The hedge-sparrow fed the cuckoo so long, that it had its head
> bit off by its young," and "Whoop jug, I know when the horse fol-
> lows the cart," are a running commentary of trite truisms, pointing
> out the extreme folly of the infatuated old monarch, and in a
> manner reconciling us to its inevitable consequences.[49]

The Fool's witty remarks *relieve, aid,* and *reconcile.*
They offer relief when the contrast between Lear's anguish and his daughter's "petrifying indifference" has
become "too painful"; but this relief, though necessary
and welcome, immediately intensifies our sympathy with
Lear. By showing, "in the most familiar point of view,"
the "pitiable weakness" of Lear's conduct and "its ir-
retrievable consequences," the Fool's wit "carries the
pathos to the highest pitch of which it is capable."[50] As
he counterpoints "on a meaner scale" Lear's catalog of
follies, the Fool helps Lear strip himself defenseless, increasing thereby our feelings of both sympathy and horror. At the same time, Hazlitt explains, the Fool's
"commentary" reconciles us to evil: not by softening its
outlines but by making us better acquainted with its
ugliness, by converting "calamity and disappointment"
into sympathy with others, and by translating knowledge
of evil into desire for good.[51] This consummation is
reached in the moment when Lear, with his pity for the
"poor naked wretches," identifies himself with the Fool
and other unfortunates. Lear and the Fool are pushed
apart by their stations in life and by their diction, but

they are pulled together by the contrapuntal import of their speeches and, finally, by Lear's recognition of their common humanity. Wit and imagination oppose each other in a tension which, when it finally breaks, helps render the coalescence indissoluble and, in both emotional power and aggregation, "sublime." In more than "light and ludicrous" works Hazlitt accepts a degree of "indifference" as appropriate to the poem's effect, even though indifference may temporarily jar the "natural" progress of association from its path to "truth." He recognizes that sometimes it is as important to control or shape emotion as it is to evoke it.

Hazlitt's principal criterion for judging poetry remains truth to nature. The truth of poetry is based on common experience, known through sympathetic identification and communicated by generally moving materials. In the greatest poetry, emotion-charged images initiate trains of association that bring the whole mind into play in a process of knowing and valuing. The consummation of this process requires intense feeling, and anything that dampens emotion checks the process. This is the effect of wit, with its "artificial" materials and incongruous comparisons. Nevertheless, although the poetry of wit inverts the order of nature, it attains its own kind of internal consistency, which is a source of aesthetic pleasure. Furthermore, although witty poetry precludes the depth of sympathetic understanding that imagination can achieve, its detachment guards against a still more serious threat to nature: mere subjectivity. As in *The Beggar's Opera,* it may be more "natural" than poetry in which the poet has identified his characters, not with general nature, but only with himself. Finally, as in *King Lear,* the poet may use the divisive method of wit as a means to ultimate coalescence and hence to the highest degree of imaginative truth.

VI

"Common Places" and Paradox

> Mr. Wordsworth is at the head of that which has been denominated the Lake school of poetry; a school which, with all my respect for it, I do not think sacred from criticism or exempt from faults, of some of which faults I shall speak with becoming frankness . . . —"On the Living Poets" (1818).

DESPITE HIS CLASSIFICATION of English poetry written between the reign of Queen Anne and the French Revolution as the "poetry of mere common places," Hazlitt applies this term only sparingly to English nondramatic poetry of the eighteenth century. Instead, his "poetry of common places" principally comprises French classical tragedy and English imitations thereof. His term "paradoxical" also extends to foreign literature, for he applies it to German tragedy as well as to most English poetry of his own time. The poetry of "common places" and the poetry of paradox are marked, respectively, by stereotyped language, situations, and characters and by personal idiosyncrasy. These two kinds of poetry are alike in being imaginatively inhibited, not, as in comedy or the poetry of wit, by demands inherent in the class but by faults that degrade a poem within its own genre. Both kinds suffer from a kind of egotism that prevents imaginative self-fulfillment.[1]

For Hazlitt the best poetry demands self-fulfillment, for both the poet and the reader, in the sense that every area of possible emotional, intellectual, and moral response must remain open to the probings of association that are initiated by concrete particulars. "Wherever an intense activity is given to any one faculty" at the expense of "the due and natural exercise of others," this imaginative fulfillment is blocked, and there occurs what has been called more recently a "dissociation of sensibility" from knowing and valuing.[2] Intellectual activity in which "ideas of things" are divorced from pleasure or pain "must check the genial expansion of the moral sentiments and social affections, [and] lead to a cold and dry abstraction." When an object or idea is severed from its association with pain or pleasure, as it must be in scientific or syllogistic reasoning, it is devaluated as material for poetry. For both poet and reader, the concrete particular, with its immediate emotional impact, must be allowed to initiate and enrich the flow of associations —especially those resulting from sympathetic identification—that modify perception and shape poetic truth. Other exclusive habits of mind, such as personal "vanity" or devotion to some philosophical or political scheme, have a similar effect on the imagination, excluding essential truths or preventing their expression in generally interesting images and events.[3] Since the poet must respond completely—in sensation, thought, and feeling—to the evocative experience, he must not interpose his will; he must not, like the French dramatists, begin with an "abstract thing" or impose a rigid pattern of rhetoric; he must not, like Shelley, discard "every thing as mystery and error for which he cannot account by an effort of mere intelligence," or, like Southey, lack the "patience to think that evil is inseparable from the nature of things," or, like Coleridge, "subject the Muse to *transcendental* theories."[4]

In Hazlitt, therefore, we find the same paradox as in Keats. Just as the denial of self that Keats calls negative capability must precede the affirmation of self that he calls soul-making, so must a high degree of sympathetic identification, and consequent loss of self, precede the self-fulfillment that Hazlitt defines as the poetic experience. Whether, as in Wordsworth, "egotism" makes every object in nature mirror the poet's own thoughts and feelings, or as in Godwin, uses character and passion to "spin a subtle theory," or, as in Coleridge, "mistakes scholastic speculations for the intricate windings of the passions," this egotism in poetry is "servile, inert, . . . stagnant." Keats and Hazlitt use similar metaphors to suggest the vitality and completeness of the imaginative experience when it is uninhibited by any abstracting or dividing egotism. Modern literature, says Hazlitt, "halts on one leg"; it does not—like Keats' bright-eyed, purposeful Stoat—"run on all fours." Modern poets, says Hazlitt, "are more in love with a theory than a mistress"; whereas in his "instinctiveness," says Keats, the poet should be like a Hawk or a Man "wanting a Mate." It is this absorption in a self-integrating or self-completing purpose that embodies poetic truth in striking particulars.[5] Neither Hazlitt nor, I think, Keats is insisting on the amorality of the imaginative process, not, at least, in any final sense. Douglas Bush has pointed out that what Keats opposes to "the wordsworthian or egotistical sublime" is "the impersonal, non-moral imagination of the poet of negative capability."[6] But for Hazlitt, at least, the imaginative fusion includes morality: "impassioned poetry is an emanation of the moral and intellectual part of our nature, as well as of the sensitive—of the desire to know, the will to act, and the power to feel; and ought to appeal to these different parts of our constitution, in order to be perfect."[7] This emanation must, of

course, come naturally through the process of excited
but conditioned association. Apparently it must come as
spontaneously and organically as the Ancient Mariner's
blessing of the water-snakes, an act of unpremeditated
but indisputable morality. The process of poetic creation, Hazlitt makes it clear, involves a moral response—
conditioned by sympathetic identification—that leaves
its mark on the final product, but he protests that any
premature moralizing can only obstruct the process short
of fruition.

As a political writer Hazlitt frequently objects to political ideas expressed in poems, plays, or novels; but
when he considers a piece of writing as an imaginative
work rather than a political document (and in Hazlitt's
essays the distinction is not difficult to make), his objection is not to any particular set of ideas but to a writer
allowing any ideas—political or otherwise—to control his
imagination. Although he has no use for Sir Walter
Scott's politics, he finds "the political bearing of the
Scotch Novels . . . a relief to the mind, rarified as it has
been with the modern philosophy, and heated with ul-
tra-radicalism." For Scott (usually) does not "enter into
the distinctions of hostile seats or parties" but deals with
essential qualities common to all mankind.[8] Hazlitt's
own political ideas, reduced to what Keats calls consequitive reasoning, are no more acceptable as material for
poetry than anyone else's. "The cause of the people is
indeed but little calculated as a subject for poetry: it admits of rhetoric, which goes into argument and explanation, but it presents no immediate or distinct images to
the mind. . . ." In fact, tyranny, if dramatized by striking
and powerful characters like Coriolanus, will stimulate
the imagination and prove more attractive and sympathetic than "abstract right." This does not mean, obviously, that literature must repudiate democratic ideas.

"The spirit of poetry is in itself favourable to humanity and liberty. . . ."[9] At the point where imaginative fulfillment culminates in unselfish identification—or, perhaps more accurately, unselfish identification culminates in imaginative fulfillment—Hazlitt's criteria for political and for poetic success become the same. At this point, ideally, both society and a poem achieve an organic unity correlative with the good citizen's and the poet's and the reader's self-integration. Of course, regarding the chances of reaching this ideal, Hazlitt is more sanguine about poetry than about society, although in his own time, he thought, poetry also faced some pretty serious difficulties.

i

The limitations that the poetry of "common places" has imposed on imaginative fulfillment result, in some cases, from indolent recourse to hackneyed diction but also, more grievously, from allowing reason to override the imagination. James Thomson illustrates the first of these faults. Hazlitt admires Thomson ("the best of our descriptive poets") for his massing of details ("No one has yet come up to him in giving the sum total of their effects") and for his total involvement ("He describes not to the eye alone, but to the other senses, and to the whole man"). Apparently he gains a synaesthetic dimension as well as its moral equivalent. ". . . Thomson always gives a *moral sense* to nature."[10] But he fails to write imaginative poetry consistently, not because his reason or his vanity overrides his imagination, but because he is indolent. His blank verse is "heavy and monotonous"; and he frequently lapses into the "pedantic and ostentantious in his style. . . . He takes advantage of all the most trite and mechanical common-places of

imagery and diction . . . as if he thought them quite as
good . . . as his own poetry."

> Come, gentle Spring! ethereal Mildness! come,
> And from the bosom of yon dropping cloud,
> While music wakes around, veil'd in a shower
> Of shadowing roses, on our plains descend.

Hazlitt objects to overloading "the exquisitely natural
sentiment" of "fresh, and innocent Spring . . . descend-
ing to earth," with a "cloud of painted, pompous, cum-
brous phrases, like the shower of roses."[11] This objection,
apparently, is not to the personification or to the adjec-
tive-noun combinations but to Thomson's departure
from observable truth by bringing in the music and the
showering roses.[12] For "a set of striking images" Hazlitt
quotes the next fifteen lines of *The Seasons,* which include "surly Winter," "ruffian blasts," "howling hill,"
"shatter'd forest," "ravag'd vale," "softer gales," "kind
touch," "dissolving snows," "livid torrents," "green
heads" [of mountains], "trembling year," "pale morn,"
"driving sleets," "day delightless," "sounding marsh,"
"wild notes," and "list'ning waste."[13] Hazlitt probably
liked some of these better than others, but apparently he
did not object to the syntactical monotony of Thomson's
epithets.[14]

Hazlitt would allow poetry "a greater number of in-
versions" than occur in prose and more frequent "epithets and ornaments,"[15] but he agrees with Wordsworth
that the language of poetry should rise naturally from
the poet's feeling for his subject and that it should be
generally moving. He wants language that, representing
closely observed particulars, is richly connotative for the
general reader. If Thomson failed to achieve this kind
of language from indolence, the French dramatists and
their English imitators failed from principle. Their artificial style, cramped into pre-established patterns, and

their correlative faults of stereotyped characters and situations result from following closely reasoned principles rather than the imagination. In his essay "On Ancient and Modern Literature" in *Lectures on the Age of Elizabeth* (1820) Hazlitt defines four "sorts or schools of tragedy": (1) "the antique or classical," (2) "the Gothic or romantic," which includes the best writers of the age of Elizabeth, especially Shakespeare, (3) "the French or common-place rhetorical style," and (4) "the German or paradoxical style."[16] Of the four kinds, the third is the least tragic, for in it the sweep and intensity of feeling is most restricted. Since it is the work of "conjecture and reasoning," it never goes beyond "the general impression of the situation of the persons—beyond general reflections on the passions—beyond general descriptions of objects."[17]

Like A. W. Schlegel, whose *Lectures on Dramatic Literature* Hazlitt reviewed in the *Edinburgh Review* for 1815, Hazlitt is "extremely suspicious" of all activity in art "which originates in an abstract theory." Both Hazlitt and Schlegel trace the inferiority of French tragedy to reliance on authority rather than on "the almost unconscious and immediate contemplation of great and important truths."[18] The French simply "are not a people of imagination."[19] In French drama, impressions of nature have not been allowed to exert their full force on the poet's imagination, for his creative flow of associations has been dammed up by preconceived and generalized notions about how characters should speak, act, and feel. "The true poet transports you to the scene" so that "you catch, from the lips of the persons concerned, what lies nearest to their hearts"; but the French poets explicitly describe the passions rather than allowing the characters to reveal themselves dramatically.[20] As a result, the thought and feeling are only the poet's; the characters remain undifferentiated and unsympathized with—"didactic" rather than "dramatic"—their dialog "a tissue of common places" which could just as well be spoken by one character as another.[21] Diction and rhetoric are all part of the "given mould" into which everything must be cast. Since the language has to be "clear and defined" and "intelligible by its previous applications" (like Hobbes' language of reason), it excludes everything "obscure, distant, imperfect." The French poet shears off all the "complexity and distinctions" from the "images of things" and reduces them to a "general class or name."[22] This formal rhetoric stands in the way of truth, because imaginative fulfillment—or the immediate coalescence of an idea with concrete forms—does not fall into neat and balanced patterns. In this respect Corneille and Racine are like that other "didactic reasoner," Dr. Johnson, whose mind was affected by "the most exquisite refinement or sublimity . . . only as they could be translated into the language of measured prose."[23]

Transplanted into England after the Restoration, the artificial, "common-place" style produced unfortunate results that lasted for some time. As examples of French influence Hazlitt cites Nathaniel Lee, Congreve's tragic poetry, and Addison's *Cato*, but Dryden's plays are "perhaps the fairest specimen of what this manner was. . . . All the characters are put into a swaggering attitude of dignity, and tricked out in the pomp of ostentatious drapery. The images are extravagant, yet not far-fetched; they are outrageous caricatures of obvious thoughts: the language oscillates between bombast and bathos: the characters are noisy pretenders to virtue, and shallow boasters in vice; the versification is laboured and monotonous, quite unlike the admirably free and flowing rhyme of his satires, in which he felt the true inspiration of his subject, and could find modulated sounds to express it."[24] In the eighteenth century Dryden's successors —Smith, Hill, Hughes, Murphy, and Dr. Johnson—reduced tragedy to "the most frigid, insipid, and insignificant of all things." But the *"tragedie bourgeoise"* of Southern, Lillo, and Edward Moore was a kind of revival of the "Gothic or romantic" tragedy of the Elizabethans. "The antithesis of the classical form," it at least "went out of the established road to seek for truth and nature and effect in the commonest life and lowest situations."[25] German paradoxical tragedy—Schiller, Kotzebue, Goethe—"is an insult and defiance to Aristotle's definition of tragedy"; an indecorous, improbable, and immoral extravagance; but still a "good thing." German tragedy is not true, but its "excitement and zest" at least open the way to truth in a manner that abstract reason cannot.[26]

ii

Coming closer home, Hazlitt is not quite so tolerant when his contemporaries in England and Scotland violate decorum or veer passionately from the truth. To Hazlitt much of the poetry of his own time seemed "paradoxical" in its lawlessness and subjectivity; but usually his "poets of paradox" are the Lake School, and most often it is Wordsworth whom Hazlitt chooses to represent the paradoxical. The Lake School of poetry "had its origin in the French revolution, or rather in those sentiments and opinions which produced that revolution." It was founded "on a principle of sheer humanity, on pure nature void of art." Although always a great defender of the French Revolution, humanity, and nature, especially as the gauge of art, Hazlitt put the poetry of paradox at the bottom of a scale of excellence down which English poetry had been sliding since

the Renaissance.[27] He does not, by any means, put
Wordsworth at the bottom of the scale. He uses Wordsworth to illustrate tendencies on which he blames the
inferior position of contemporary poetry, but at the
same time he recognizes in Wordsworth a kind of imaginative power that had been lacking in English poetry
for over a century.

"The paradox [the Lake poets] set out with was, that
all things are by nature equally fit subjects for poetry;
or that if there is any preference to be given, those that
are the meanest and most unpromising are the best, as
they leave the greatest scope for the unbounded stores
of thought and fancy in the writer's own mind." It is
in this sense, not in any political one, that the paradoxical poets leveled distinctions and, in an excess of revolutionary zeal, flouted "authority and fashion."[28] Indeed,
the fact that the chief practitioners of paradox had
turned against the French Revolution, and against Hazlitt as well, may suggest that Hazlitt's evaluation of the
poetry of paradox was not entirely disinterested. This
was the view of Wordsworth, who in 1817 wrote to Haydon that "the miscreant Hazlitt continues . . . his abuse
of Southey Coleridge and myself." A hundred years later Hazlitt's old enemy *Blackwood's Magazine* asserted
the "whimsical paradox" that "Hazlitt, a Jacobin in politics, was a violent anti-Jacobin in literature."[29] This
proposition is acceptable only if "anti-Jacobin" is adequately defined. The *Blackwood's* article proceeds to
confuse Hazlitt's literary anti-Jacobinism with the abuse
of "Wordsworth's private character," but the paradoxes
in Hazlitt's position may be resolved without recourse
to his personal or political disputes: Hazlitt is not guilty
of his own charge against the "Ministerial Press" of making "literature the mere tool . . . of party-spirit,"[30] nor
is he repudiating the French Revolution, humanity, or
nature.

Hazlitt's dislike for Wordsworth's and Coleridge's politics is distinguishable from his evaluation of their poetry, just as his attacks on Scott the Tory are distinct from his admiration of Scott the novelist. Although he singled out the paradoxical elements for disapproval, Hazlitt admired a great deal of Wordsworth's poetry; in fact, he placed Wordsworth "decidedly at the head of the poets of the present day, or rather . . . in a totally distinct class of excellence." Hazlitt, as Wellek has pointed out, recognized "the best of his time remarkably well"; and shortly after Hazlitt's death T. N. Talfourd could write in the *Examiner* that, despite his personal bitterness toward Wordsworth and Coleridge, only Hazlitt "has done justice to the immortal works of the one, and the genius of the other."[31] Although we no longer find it as difficult as the Victorians did to respect Hazlitt, it is nevertheless pleasant to note how firm Hazlitt's critical principles stood against political pressure and personal abuse.

Hazlitt's literary anti-Jacobinism affirms, rather than rejects, his own political ideas. Probably better than any other part of his critical writings, Hazlitt's analysis of the poetry of paradox, especially Wordsworth's, shows his belief that the good poet, like the good citizen, must fulfill the possibilities of his imagination: that poetic structure, like the best government, requires an escape from egotism into imaginative completeness. This principle is the key to Hazlitt's criticism of Wordsworth and other contemporaries. Occasionally, when Hazlitt expresses this principle in the commonplace terms of logic, decorum, and general nature, he may seem to apply it too harshly and mechanically; more often, however, the criterion of imaginative completeness leads Hazlitt to appreciate Wordsworth's excellence and to censure—in Wordsworth and others—what may justifiably be con-

sidered idiosyncrasy, bathos, and structural ineptitude.
Hazlitt may sometimes, like many of his contemporaries,
blur the distinctions between art and nature, but in his
treatment of the poetry of paradox he takes a clear stand
against subjectivism and formlessness, and insists that
poetry attain a structured objectivity.

iii

Hazlitt's general charge against the poets of his time
is that they have gone to such extremes of subjectivity
that they have failed to achieve either (1) a high degree
of truth, (2) the means of poetic communication, or (3)
both. Everywhere he finds a perverse individuality.
Southey's "impressions are accidental, immediate, personal, instead of being permanent and universal." Shelley "trusted too implicitly to the light of his own mind."
Keats, in *Endymion,* "painted his own thoughts and
character." Byron is a "pampered egotist" who, instead
of bowing "to the authority of nature, . . . only consults
the . . . workings of his own breast, and gives them out
as oracles to the world." Landor's *Imaginary Conversations* is "a *chef-d'œuvre* of self-opinion and self-will."
Landor and, to a lesser degree, Southey are the principal
examples of that extreme form of paradox that Hazlitt
calls "Literary Jacobinism." Hazlitt has a number of
good things to say about the style, characterization, and
humor in the *Imaginary Conversations,* but all is "de-
faced" by Landor's outrageous love of paradox that offends both reason and common sense.[32] At this point,
Hazlitt's criticism of the poetry of paradox approaches a
kind of commonplace logic-chopping, but his main concern is that the poets of paradox failed to consummate
the imaginative process that great poetry exacts.

The greatest poetry, Hazlitt believes, must objectify
thought and feeling in generally moving images and ex-

citing events. In a state of intense feeling the imagination shapes the poet's experience into a work of art, selecting and combining those particulars that reflect the order of nature and stimulate the reader's imagination to realize what is permanent and meaningful in human life. Reviewing *The Excursion* in 1814, Hazlitt divides poetry into "two classes; the poetry of imagination and the poetry of sentiment." The first arises "out of the faculties of memory and invention, conversant with the world of external nature; the other from the fund of our moral sensibility."[33] Here Hazlitt uses the term "poetry of imagination" in a narrower sense than he usually does, for he apparently wants to emphasize the objectifying or externalizing power of imagination, its ability to fuse thoughts and feelings with concrete particulars. More frequently, as in describing Shakespeare's or Milton's poetry, he makes the "poetry of imagination" include high moral sensibility as well as excellent invention. In fact, in his review of *The Excursion,* he goes on to say that "the greatest poets . . . have been equally distinguished for richness of invention and depth of feeling." Since the days of Chaucer, Spenser, Shakespeare, and Milton the decline of poetry can be traced to the failure to combine "moral sensibility" and "fanciful invention." Young and Cowley possess the latter but not the former. ". . . Wordsworth, on the other hand, whose powers of feeling are of the highest order, is certainly deficient in fanciful invention: his writings exhibit all the internal power, without the external form of poetry."[34]

iv

As we have seen, Hazlitt's objection to Shelley's and Southey's use of political ideas is that, by beginning with the idea, these poets set up an insuperable barrier to

imaginative fulfillment. Wordsworth, too, sometimes
stopped short of the kind of imaginative completeness
that Hazlitt seeks in literature, but this is because he ex-
cessively delighted in "contemplating his own powers"
rather than because any set of political ideas intervened.
Wordsworth, of course, was no less aware than Hazlitt
of the problems that the times imposed on a poet, and if
he "contemplated his own powers," it was in order to
solve one of the most difficult of these problems. Defining "the triumph of the mechanical philosophy," Basil
Willey has noted that by the eighteenth century poets
felt that "mythologies, including the Christian, were . . .
exploded," that their "truth," as far as it goes, could be
stated conceptually (as in the *Essay on Man*), and that
they could no longer be used in poetry except as recognized " 'fictions' of proved evocative power and of long
association with poetic experience" (as in *The Rape of
the Lock*). A major poet, therefore, forced by his concern for truth to deny the old mythologies, had either
(like Keats and Shelley, often) to invent a new mythology, although not necessarily discarding all of the old, or
(like Wordsworth) to "make poetry out of the direct
dealings of his mind and heart with the visible universe.
. . ."[35] But if Wordsworth rejected the mythology that
had been rejected by scientific thought, he also rejected
(although not fully) the explanatory method of Pope's
philosophical poems. In a good many places, including
a passage in *The Excursion* (IV, 941-992) which Hazlitt
quotes with approval, Wordsworth says that no abstractions should come between the poet and the sensory
world which he molds to his thoughts and feelings.
Hazlitt gives Wordsworth credit for the "immediate intercourse of [his] imagination with Nature" and his repudiation of the "cold, narrow, lifeless spirit of modern
philosophy." "Tintern Abbey" (lines 76-83) shows how

"a fine poet . . . describes the effect of the sight of nature
on his mind"; and Hazlitt adds praise in what are un-
questionably his highest terms: "So the forms of nature
. . . stood before the great artists of old. . . ." This is the
reason why Wordsworth's "general sentiments and reflections" attain depth, originality, and truth.[36]

The point at which "abstraction" drains the power
from Wordsworth's poetry is that at which "vanity" or
"egotism" limits his invention to those images, characters, and incidents that are interesting only to himself
or, perhaps, other "retired and lonely student[s] of nature."[37] This is a failure in sympathetic identification.
Shakespeare and Milton, through the completeness of
their identification with others, made their images, characters, and incidents meaningful and moving to a large
number of readers. Wordsworth's materials, on the other hand, do not touch off such splendid associations. At
one extreme, Hazlitt—always empirical—brings the
"mysticism" of the Immortality Ode down to earth with
a few common-sense observations, although elsewhere
he quotes some lines of this poem approvingly. As might
be expected, he very often is unsympathetic with the
"dim, obscure, and visionary" in Coleridge (although
liking parts of "Christabel" and proclaiming "The Ancient Mariner" "a work of genius");[38] but, as far as
Wordsworth is concerned, his usual objection is at the
other extreme: to those materials that are ordinary and
unpoetic. Vain Wordsworth will "owe nothing but to
himself" and therefore abjures "figures," "fantasies,"
"the georgeous machinery of mythologic lore," "the
splendid colors of poetic diction," "striking subjects,"
and "remarkable combinations of events" in favor of
"the simplest elements of nature and the human mind,"
"the commonest events and objects," trifling "incidents," "the most insignificant things," and those ob-

jects "the most simple and barren of effect." As one
might expect, these "objects (whether persons or
things)" do not "immediately and irresistibly . . . convey
[his feelings] in all their force and depth to others. . . ."[39]

Up to a point, with his emphasis on common experience and general associations, Hazlitt is merely making
the same objection to Wordsworth that Jeffrey made in
his review of *The Excursion* in November 1814. In his
Encyclopaedia Britannica article on "Beauty" (1824),
which is an expanded version of his May 1811 review of
Archibald Alison's *Essays on the Nature and Principles
of Taste,* Jeffrey agrees with Alison and others that
beauty depends not on a thing itself but on the affections
and sympathies that we associate with it. For the *enjoyment* of beauty, therefore, the best taste—which is the
awareness of the most beauty—belongs to the person
whose affections are so warm and so much exercised that
he builds up a multiplicity of pleasurable associations.
But Jeffrey is not content with mere subjectivism in art.
The *creation* of beauty for others to enjoy requires the
poet or artist "to employ only such objects as are the
natural signs, or the *inseparable* concomitants of emotions, of which the greater part of mankind are suscept-
ible." If, instead, he intrudes objects not commonly
associated with any interesting impressions, he is guilty
of "bad and false" taste. This is Wordsworth's principal
defect, resulting, no doubt, from "long habits of seclu-
sion, and an excessive ambition of originality."[40]

Jeffrey's appeal to the susceptibility of "common
minds" does not, regardless of the quality of those
minds, set a very sophisticated standard of taste. Art,
Jeffrey is saying, offers pleasure like that associated with
certain objects in actual life but lacks, or at least makes
no use of, an order or truth peculiar to itself. As Wellek
points out, "Jeffrey and his models . . . have no criterion

to set off enjoyment of a peaceful landscape, or sudden insight into character from experience derived from art objects."[41] Hazlitt frequently invites the same criticism. His highest praise for Shakespeare's characters, for instance, is that we know them as we know real persons or that we can completely identify ourselves with them. As we have seen, he fuses the social and the aesthetic effects of tragedy. He does not, like Coleridge, separate "the Good" and "the Beautiful."[42]

The importance of how a poet combines and organizes his value-charged materials is nevertheless something that Hazlitt was aware of. Although *The Excursion* "excites or recals the same sensations which those who have traversed that wonderful scenery must have felt," Hazlitt adds that "all is left loose and irregular in the rude chaos of aboriginal nature." The cause of this poor construction is egotism: that great fault of the poets of paradox. Wordsworth has merely recorded his own experience—his own sensations and his accompanying feelings and thoughts. The result is not only "nakedness" (of commonplace, undercharged materials) but also "confusion." Wordsworth's structural faults—like the "tendency of [his] mind"—are "the reverse of the dramatic."[43] *The Excursion* lacks what is most important to a dramatic poem—that is, a suitable action or series of actions. Carrying his originality to an egotistical extreme, Wordsworth has sacrificed narrative; whereas Scott, forced by his lack of invention to draw on tradition, always "selects a story . . . sure to please."[44] Wordsworth would have done better to make the poem completely a "philosophic" one unencumbered by narrative and description which only "hinder the progress and effect of the general reasoning." Evidently Hazlitt thinks that a logical sequence of propositions would be a better unifying principle than broken narrative that "shuns the common 'vantage-grounds of popular story, of striking incident, or fatal catastrophe." Hazlitt likes generally exciting incidents for the same reason that he values generally interesting images and characters: that is, as particulars that will stimulate the reader into imaginative creation. But also Hazlitt thinks of a series of exciting events as central in a poem's structure and, for the best poetry, even indispensable. A painting or a statue can harmonize its varied particulars within the limits of plane or solid geometry, but a poem adds the dimension of time; and to propel the reader's imagination along this axis, a sequence of exciting actions is the most effective means. Unlike the painter or sculptor, the poet must translate "the object [he describes] into some other form, which is the language of metaphor or imagination; as narrative can only interest by a succession of events and a conflict of hopes and fears."[45] Of course Hazlitt admires a number of poems, including a good many of Wordsworth's, which progress through time with little or no narrative; but for Hazlitt, as for Dr. Johnson, the highest sort of invention is narrative and dramatic, with diversified characters clashing in "remarkable combinations of events."[46] Hazlitt puts a premium on action as providing particulars both individually interesting and collectively propulsive. But he is not so much interested in a closely knit plot as in a luxuriant texture of feeling. Hazlitt admires Scott's impersonal materials and his ability to combine them in an interesting story, but he finds Scott lacking in "the intensity of feeling" that "melts and moulds" a novel into "sublimity and beauty."[47] Action must provide not only suspense but emotional force that helps integrate all the parts of a poem, play, or novel into a work of art. Apparently Hazlitt would have agreed with Matthew Arnold that "the eternal objects of poetry . . . are actions," that suitable

actions "more powerfully appeal to the great human affections," and that a "great" action so dominates a poem
with the "feeling of its situations" that it precludes any
"detached impressions" or "personal peculiarities."[48]

Broken, undercharged, non-propulsive narrative is
of course not the only undramatic sin that Hazlitt traces
to Wordsworth's egotism. With "a fastidious antipathy
to immediate effect," Wordsworth intrudes into *The
Excursion* not only his interpretation of particulars that
should not need interpretation but also superfluous particulars that "hang as a dead weight upon the imagination." There is, furthermore, "no dramatic distinction
of character." "The recluse, the pastor, and the pedlar,
are three persons in one poet." Hence, because he ascribes the same sort of imaginative coloring of natural objects to all his characters, in this poem and others as well,
Wordsworth offends with dramatic impropriety. Hazlitt
is willing to accept this coloring or molding as long as
Wordsworth does not try to pass it off as some character's rather than his own, but Hazlitt loses faith when
Wordsworth makes "pedlars and ploughmen his heroes
and . . . interpreters." Swallowed up by his own feelings,
Wordsworth's materials lack variety and contrast. The
unity of *The Excursion* lies in "an endless continuity of
feeling"—Wordsworth's own—and not in the control of
varied materials. The sort of "whole" which Wordsworth "cannot form"—but which Hazlitt prefers—is one
that preserves great variety, comprising "all the bustle,
machinery, and pantomine of the stage, or of real life."[49]
But the stage and real life are not the same thing, and in
an analysis of Hazlitt's criticism both comparisons must
be taken into account. Hazlitt rarely lets us forget that
he loved the theater—where, of course, he reviewed plays
for the *Champion*, the *Examiner*, the *Morning Chronicle*, and *The Times*—but his liking for the dramatic is of

one piece with his theory of the imagination. Since imaginative fulfillment depends on a self-denying sympathy, a work of art should break free from self-regard and gain an existence as independent as possible of the purely personal. Invention succeeds as egotism dwindles and as the poet himself appears to drop out altogether, no longer coming between an image, an action, or a character and the reader. Imaginative fulfillment externalizes itself in a form in which the organic and the dramatic match each other and become one as the imaginative process reaches a consummation.

In "Laodamia" (published in 1815 and first mentioned by Hazlitt in 1824 as one of Wordsworth's "later philosophical productions") Hazlitt finds Wordsworth a better craftsman than in *The Excursion*. "Laodamia" is of course a narrative with dialog, but to explain the poem's structure Hazlitt must obviously look for something other than a succession of lively incidents. ". . . the texture of the thoughts has the smoothness and solidity of marble."[50] In fact, Hazlitt decides that "Laodamia" succeeds in the manner of sculpture or painting, for he applies to the poem a term that he generally reserves for the visual arts: "the ideal." The ideal comprises essential qualities of an object or a person as represented not in the general terms of the reason but in the particulars seized upon by the imagination in a state of intense feeling. It is "the abstraction of any thing [not from its individuality but] from all the circumstances that weaken its effect, or lessen our admiration of it." It includes, among its conditions, balance, harmony, and repose; consequently it "rejects as much as possible not only the petty, the mean, and disagreeable, but also the agony and violence of passion, the force of contrast, and the extravagance of imagination." Poetry, however, can make good use of these latter qualities; for the poet in translating the object of his imagination into some other form has no choice but a progression through time, for which nothing is better than "a succession of events and a conflict of hopes and fears." Therefore the ideal character, reposing unchanged in harmony, is a handicap to a poet or novelist, providing only "a succession of actions without passion." Hazlitt, as usual, prefers "interesting and dramatic characters" (Shakespeare's), who are "men and not angels." Sculpture and painting must remain the "strong-hold" of the ideal. Yet *in addition* to dynamic progress through varied incidents, the greatest poetry—tragedy—achieves the steady balance of the ideal in "the superiority of character to fortune and circumstances, or the larger scope of thought and feeling thrown into it, that redeems it from the charge of vulgar grossness or physical horrors."[51] Hazlitt finds "permanent tragedy" in the equipoise of "pride of intellect and power . . . confronting and enduring pain" that Milton has given Satan and again in the "feeling of stoical indifference" that Wordsworth achieves in "Laodamia."

> Know, virtue were not virtue, if the joys
> Of sense were able to return as fast
> And surely as they vanish. Earth destroys
> Those raptures duly: *Erebus disdains—*
> *Calm pleasures there abide, majestic pains.*[52]

The speaker, Protesiláus, is obviously an ideal character, but Hazlitt's only adverse comments on this poem are on "some poorness in the diction, and some indistinctness in the images" (both unspecified). "The greater part of [the poem] might be read aloud in Elysium" for the enjoyment of "departed heroes and sages"; and Hazlitt would as soon have written the line "Elysian beauty, melancholy grace" "as have carved a Greek statue."[53] Yet, in the context of Hazlitt's total criticism of

Wordsworth and his overall admiration for the dramatic, the structure of "Laodamia"—whereby Wordsworth
objectifies his feelings in the static balance of painting
and sculpture—scarcely represents a major triumph.

To summarize: the paradoxical, or egotistical, in
Wordsworth results not only in materials sometimes
lacking general interest, but also in several structural
defects: intrusive interpretation and other superfluous
interpolations, dramatic impropriety, indistinct characterization, monotony (rather than variety in unity), and
actions less than large and controlling. Wordsworth's
structural success in "Laodamia" remains of a different
order from that which Hazlitt usually admires in poetry.

v

Nevertheless, insofar as Hazlitt deals with specific
poems, his criticism of Wordsworth is more favorable
than otherwise. Howe's index to the *Works* lists thirty-
two of Wordsworth's poems by title.[54] Of these, Hazlitt
praises eight (six without reservation), favorably quotes
six more, expresses disapproval of nine (five of them
only for their political sentiments), takes a divided view
of one, and quotes or mentions eight more without any
clear evaluation—except, of course, that he apparently
thought them worth quoting or mentioning. In addition, among those poems of which "it is not possible to
speak in terms of too high praise," Hazlitt includes (in
his 1818 lecture "On the Living Poets") "several of the
Sonnets, and a hundred others of inconceivable beauty,
of perfect originality and pathos."[55]

Among the poems that Hazlitt criticizes adversely,
The Excursion is the only one that he deals with at any
length, in the review (appearing in three issues of the
Examiner, August to October 1814) that I have already
discussed. In 1816 he briefly mentions "Simon Lee,"

along with "ideot boys and mad mothers," to suggest
the meanness of Wordsworth's materials. This also
seems to be his objection, in 1821, to "The Leech-gatherer" ("Resolution and Independence"), although, like
other critics from Coleridge on, he greatly admired parts
of this poem; and in 1817, as we have seen, he found
fault with the "mysticism" in the Immortality Ode.[56]
In the remaining poems in this group—"Gipsies," the
sonnet "November, 1813," the Thanksgiving Ode, and
the sonnets on Schill and Hofer—Hazlitt finds evidence
of Wordsworth's apostasy and is characteristically scorn-
ful of such support for the ruling class and "legitimacy."[57] His comments on these five poems all follow
Napoleon's defeat at Waterloo in June 1815 and, except for one mention of the Hofer and Schill sonnets in
1828 (when Hazlitt was working on his *Life of Napoleon*), they fall within Hazlitt's most active period as a
political writer (from his reply to "Vetus" in November
1813 to the publication of *Political Essays* in 1819).

   Although, as Talfourd reports, Hazlitt was "staggered
under the blow" of Napoleon's defeat, the succeeding
months and years find him as resolute as ever, in a time
when such resolution was far from safe, in attacking the
divine right of kings, the Congress of Vienna, the hanging of John Cashman for his part in the Spa-Fields riot,
the reduction of the Poor Rates, Castlereagh, Canning,
Malthus, Gifford, and, on political grounds, his onetime
friends and fellow-revolutionaries Coleridge, Wordsworth, and Southey. If these attacks seem severe, we
must recall the political climate in which Wordsworth,
in his Thanksgiving Ode (1816), could praise an aggressive Deity for his "pure intent" worked out in "Man—
arrayed for mutual slaughter" and Southey could write
in 1817: "We are in danger of an insurrection of the
Yahoos:—it is the fault of the governments that such a

cast [*sic*] should exist in the midst of civilized society, but till the breed can be mended it must be curbed, & that too with a strong hand."[58] It was during this period that the Tory periodicals, the *Quarterly* and *Blackwood's,* responded to Hazlitt's attack on the government with vicious and libelous abuse and that, at Wordsworth's request, Hazlitt was excluded from the gatherings at Lamb's. Wordsworth also took some pains to spread the report of a sexual adventure of Hazlitt's that had taken place near Keswick in 1803.[59] Writing to John Scott on 11 June 1816, in a passage omitted from *The Letters of William and Dorothy Wordsworth,* Wordsworth mentioned that he had told Haydon of the 1803 incident, and concluded that Hazlitt is "a man of low propensities, & of bad heart. . . . His sensations are too corrupt to allow him to understand my Poetry—though his ingenuity might enable him so to write as if he knew something about it."[60] In the 7 April 1817 letter already quoted (p. 128 above) Wordsworth urged Haydon "not to associate with the Fellow, he is not a proper person to be admitted into respectable society, being the most perverse and malevolent Creature that ill luck has ever thrown in my way. Avoid him—hic niger est—And this, I understand, is the general opinion wherever he is known in London."[61] One can understand the relish with which, in his lecture "On the Living Poets" (1818), Hazlitt said that Wordsworth's

egotism is in some respects a madness. . . . He hates all science and all art; he hates chemistry, he hates conchology; he hates Voltaire; he hates Sir Isaac Newton; he hates wisdom; he hates wit; he hates metaphysics, which he says are unintelligible, and yet he would be thought to understand them; he hates prose; he hates all poetry but his own; he hates the dialogues in Shakespeare; he hates music, dancing, and painting; he hates Rubens, he hates Rembrandt; he hates Raphael, he hates Titian; he hates Vandyke; he hates the antique; he hates the Apollo Belvidere; he hates the Venus of

Medicis. This is the reason that so few people take an interest in his writings, because he takes an interest in nothing that others do!

Yet it is in this same lecture that Hazlitt has only the highest praise for more than a "hundred" of Wordsworth's poems; and seven years later, in *The Spirit of the Age,* where he makes his usual high evaluation of much of Wordsworth's poetry but with particular appreciation of "his later philosophic productions," Hazlitt refers to his earlier list of Wordsworth's hates as "mere epigrams and *jeux-d'esprit,* as far from truth as they are free from malice."[62]

In "The Thorn," the "Mad Mother" ("Her eyes are wild"), and "The Complaint of a Poor Indian Woman" *(sic),* Hazlitt found, when Coleridge read these poems aloud to him in January 1798, "that deeper power and pathos which have since been acknowledged . . . as the characteristics of [the] author." At least this is the discovery that Hazlitt affirmed in "My First Acquaintance with Poets" (1823). In 1818 he also listed the "Complaint" among those others of Wordsworth's poems of which "it is not possible to speak in terms of too high praise": "Hart-Leap Well," "The Banks of the Wye" ("Tintern Abbey"), "The Reverie of Poor Susan," parts of "The Leech-gatherer," "To a Cuckoo" *(sic),* and "To a Daisy" *(sic)* (which may be any of the three poems Wordsworth called "To the Daisy" but which, because all the other poems referred to in "On the Living Poets" had been published by 1807, is probably one of the two poems of this title that appeared in the 1807 edition, although the one in the 1815 edition cannot be ruled out). "Hart-Leap Well" seems to be Hazlitt's favorite, with "Laodamia" later becoming a close competitor.[63]

In all of these, we may infer, Hazlitt discovered not only profound thoughts and sentiments but also a satisfactory degree of "fanciful invention." Five of these poems—"The Thorn," "Her eyes were wild," "The Complaint," "Hart-Leap Well," and "Laodamia"—are dramatic in that each deals with a tense, crucial situation and that the speakers, except in a very minor way in "Hart-Leap Well," are not the poet himself; all five have a distinct narrative element; and all have vivid and splendid or awesome imagery. Apparently—in 1798 and again in 1823—Hazlitt did not consider "The Thorn" and "Her eyes were wild" irreparably damaged by psychotic mothers or "a little muddy pond." In "Hart-Leap Well" Wordsworth, it seems, has found a suitable story— somewhat like Scott's material—to dramatize the thought and sentiment expressed in the last stanza (with what, according to Hazlitt's standards, one might consider an excess of interpretation and, indeed, interpretation that is not adequately prepared for dramatically). Hazlitt's reasons for admiring "Laodamia" have already been examined. The parts of "The Leech-gatherer" that pleased Hazlitt can only be guessed at: perhaps he felt, in the measured cheerfulness of the old man, something of the reposeful "ideal" that he discovered in "Laodamia";[64] probably he liked the sentiment and some of the imagery, but not the inelegant details ("muddy water" again). The old man is scarcely of lower station than the "poor Indian woman" (although, a local product, he may seem more commonplace), but his situation is less immediately dramatic, the poem's narrative interest is slight, and characterization remains indistinct (as Charles Williams notes, the Leech-gatherer seems to be "the impersonated thought of some other state of being, which the acceptance of the noble doctrine it teaches leaves in itself unexplored").[65]

F. W. Bateson points out that in "Tintern Abbey," written later than any other poem in the first edition of *Lyrical Ballads*, "Wordsworth (practically for the

first time) speaks the language that he was afterwards
to speak in prose and in verse. . . . With its long sentences, its involved grammar and its polysyllabic vo-
cabulary it was a form of discourse that abandoned all
pretense to being the poetry of the people."[66] The poet,
however, is still molding sensory experience to his own
feelings, and it is for this accomplishment that Hazlitt
especially admires the poem and places Wordsworth in
"a totally distinct class of excellence." Wordsworth has
become openly autobiographical, and the analysis of his
own mental processes has become as important as the
details of external nature.[67] But of course the poem
escapes the excesses of paradox: in ascribing these sensations, thoughts, and feelings to himself and Dorothy,
Wordsworth does not commit any dramatic impropriety; more than in the Immortality Ode he keeps his
consolation for the loss of youth's "dizzy raptures" within empirical (if not entirely logical) limits; and, to be
sure, no mud puddles or molehills devalue the banks of
the Wye as material for poetry.

We may only infer Hazlitt's reasons for mentioning the remaining three poems favorably; and for lack
of specific evidence, these inferences must be brief.
"The Reverie of Poor Susan," although not published
until 1800, was written before "Tintern Abbey" and is
a kind of preliminary sketch for it. It avoids the first
person; and its concrete particulars are appropriate to
the character (therefore "dramatic" and not merely
"picturesque"). The poem has a clear chronological
structure, with its parts neatly describing successive
stages of the process of association: the initiating bird
song, the delightful recall of pleasing images, and their
subsequent fading away. "To the Cuckoo" is a first-person lyric with a good deal of generally appealing concrete detail; the imagery is given texture by the basic

metaphor (the bird is a "Voice" suggesting "an unsubstantial, faery" world). A very similar case could be made for the 1807 daisy poem beginning "In youth from rock to rock," while the other daisy poem of that year, beginning "Bright Flower," although less concrete is closely structured and is a good example of unmuddied Nature imaginatively molded to express profound sentiments.

vi

Hazlitt's favorite thesis, that imaginative activity has steadily declined since Shakespeare and Milton, forced him to put the poetry of paradox at the bottom of his scale, but his evaluation of Wordsworth's individual poems is usually a high one. Despite personal and political animosity, Hazlitt recognizes the imaginative power of Wordsworth's "immediate intercourse" with sensory nature, his consequent kinship with "the great artists of old," and his unique excellence in his own time.

But this imaginative excellence, Hazlitt believes, has been pulled up short of fulfillment, and therefore lacks the dramatic invention that the greatest poetry requires. If Hazlitt's estimate of Wordsworth is high, it is also discriminating. Wordsworth shares the fault that, in general at least, gives his contemporaries the lowest place on Hazlitt's scale. Hazlitt's case against contemporary poetry rests on the various kinds of egotism that perverted reason or—what is more important to Hazlitt—blocked the imagination. He objects to the "literary Jacobinism" of Landor and Southey, to the intrusion of political ideas by Shelley and Godwin and of metaphysics by Coleridge, to Wordsworth's choice of materials remote from general experience and interest, and to the structural defects of paradox: interpretation, needless interpolation, dramatic impropriety, lack of variety, and slightness of action. Hazlitt nevertheless takes account of Wordsworth's "ideal" but undramatic structure in "Laodamia." Hazlitt's ideas of structure are obviously less sophisticated and less comprehensive than those that have become current in this century, but they are sound and fundamental.

Hazlitt is always searching literature for the kind of truth that duplicates nature; but, at the same time, his respect for the truth of nature (imaginatively molded, but undistorted by the merely personal) leads to his high regard for the kind of poetry that has broken free from the poet himself. This freedom is most complete when the structure is most completely dramatic. There is nothing contradictory in this emphasis on both the truth of nature and poetic structure. The poet's imagination can embrace the truth of nature only when unhampered by any sort of egotism, for truth requires complete self-fulfillment—intellectual, emotional, and moral—and, if the process of association leading to this fulfillment is blocked by preconceived ideas or other forms of self-regard, the highest truth will not be attained. Thus the process of imagination and artistic creation proceeds simultaneously toward two goals, each dependent on the other: the completeness of self-fulfillment and its counterpart in organic yet objective form wherein "profound sentiments" are realized in images, characters, and incidents of the most pleasing and striking kind. Only then is the poet's invention rich enough to embody profound sentiments.

Nor is there any inconsistency between Hazlitt's revolutionary political doctrine and his repudiation of this doctrine as material for poetry. *Any* doctrine, egotistically insisted on, aborts the imaginative completeness that Hazlitt makes the basis of both aesthetic and political achievement. Successful literature, therefore, cannot help being politically and socially useful, and there can be no basic conflict between humanitarian goals and poetic achievement. If Hazlitt is guilty of a paradox, it is one that his job as a political writer made difficult to avoid, for the urgency of writing on current issues puts negative capability to a bitter test. Of course, negative capability is a condition of imaginative writing only; but Hazlitt's political essays are rarely, if ever, addressed to consequitive reasoners. Since, to combat the "cold, philosophic indifference" of his opponents,[68] Hazlitt exploits all the resources of literature, his political writings become imaginative works into which he rushes with ideas as demonstratively preconceived as Shelley's and Southey's.

Yet, as positive as Hazlitt may be on basic principles, almost the whole body of his political writing aims at the negation of political actions that he thought would further restrict the people's rights. He opposed Poor-Law reform, for instance, because—inadequate as the Poor Laws were—he believed that in the current political atmosphere of selfishness and greed any legislative action would hurt the working classes more than it would help them. In the meantime, he thought, he could do no more in a practical way than to stand off further wrongs. Politically as well as aesthetically, he urges disinterestedness: the sympathetic identification that is needed for imaginative fulfillment. This is clear in Hazlitt's political writings. Among his critical essays it is clearest in his criticism of Wordsworth, the chief poet of paradox.

VII

Style and Structure

> The proper force of words lies not in the words
> themselves, but in their application.—"On Fa-
> miliar Style" (1821).

AFTER THE SUCCESS of *Table-Talk,* contributed to John
Scott's *London Magazine* in 1820, Hazlitt's essays fall increasingly into the category known as "familiar," although he had been writing and publishing essays of this
kind since 1813.[1] Hazlitt's familiar essays are not, of
course, distinguished from his earlier work by any clear
change in subject matter. In them we still find his long-
standing ideas on literature and art, on politics, and on
the workings of the human mind, but these ideas tend
to be more completely assimilated to "the world of men
and women, . . . their actions, . . . motives, . . . whims,
. . . pursuits, . . . absurdities, [and] inconsistencies."[2]
There are further differences. Although Hazlitt never
achieved a high degree of negative capability, much less
the dramatic form that marks its culmination, he made
an approach to both. In the essays after 1820, Hazlitt
is less aggressive in asserting his convictions; his tone is
less strident, more tolerant, more aphoristic. His "dark
and doubtful views" are less immediately provoked by
the political situation. His style, now completely his
own, has become a flexible instrument for his thought
and feeling. As his mood requires, his style is simple or
elaborate, dryly colloquial or richly figurative. Ideas

that once resisted statement attain clarity and precision. In his earlier work, Hazlitt's efforts to clarify abstract propositions often drove him into desperate convolutions, but in the rich essays of his last decade, where he is not so much concerned with consequitive reasoning, he puts his turns of thought and feeling to good use. Although Hazlitt's basic ideas remain the same, he has gradually learned to express them—as he thought all ideas should be expressed—imaginatively.

An account of Hazlitt and the creative imagination would not be complete without an examination of the imaginative qualities of Hazlitt's own writing. His prose is frequently rich with *imagery* in his own sense of the word—that is, with concrete particulars which have expressive associations. Hazlitt also wrote a dry style, relatively bare of images, crisply idiomatic and sometimes ironical. Although this style may occasionally dominate a paragraph or even an essay, it is usually not prolonged. Hazlitt's feelings were too strong, and the resulting associations too abundant, for him to sustain a style either concise or detached. In many of his best essays his crisp style is interwoven with his more imaginative style into an intricate design of varying moods. Hazlitt says that his essays are poorly constructed, but his best ones testify to the power of emotion to channel associations into a unified pattern. His structures—syntactic and larger—are not the result of formal planning but are what Hazlitt would call "discursive" as opposed to "consecutive."[3] They frequently employ symmetrical elements, but these are likely to merge into a larger asymmetrical design. To use the inevitable Romantic figure, they are not mechanically contrived but have grown organically. They are the product of a free but disciplined imagination.

i

The prose essay, as Hazlitt defines it, is a work of the imagination. In applying Hazlitt's own criteria to his own work, we should begin with his critical statements about the kind of writing that he himself attempted. His comments on prose style are numerous, the longest and most systematic being one of his *Table-Talk* essays, "On Familiar Style."[4] To write the familiar style, says Hazlitt, is "not to take the first word that offers, but the best word in common use; it is not to throw words together in any combinations we please, but to follow and avail ourselves of the true idiom of the language." This is not a "random" style or one that is "easy to write." It demands rigorous precision in selecting and combining words free from eccentric or jarring tones and appropriate to the writer's total meaning. The familiar style gains "universal force" by eschewing the pedantic, the pompous, the disgusting, the obsolete or archaic, the hyperbolic, the commonplace, the merely technical or professional, the cant or slang phrase, the newly coined word, and the *"slipshod* allusion."[5] In order to "clench a writer's meaning," moreover, each word must be "fitted . . . to its place" in the whole structure of a work. This selection and arrangement cannot be achieved according to any "mechanical rule or theory": it is an act of the imagination requiring a "fine tact"—a practiced ear and an identifying sympathy. Hazlitt offers the analogy of reading aloud. One's ability "to give the true accent and inflection to the words" is determined by "the habitual associations between sense and sound, and . . . by entering into the author's meaning." Similarly a habitual sensitivity to language and a continual awareness of the total effect must guide a writer to a "spontaneous" choice and arrangement of words.[6] Although it seems

that Hazlitt himself did little revising,[7] he explains the
apparently conflicting demands of spontaneity and care-
ful revision. He does not agree with Cobbett "that the
first word that occurs is always the best," but he insists
that if a better word is to be found, as it often may be,
"it should be suggested naturally . . . and spontaneously,
from a fresh and lively conception of the subject." During revision the imaginative process must be allowed to
start up again "by touching some link in the chain of
previous association" and reach a point where the pattern of the whole work is clearly grasped.[8] The universality of the imaginative style is a matter not only of language charged with thought and feeling but of words
linked to each other by associations based on much experience and consequently reflecting the order of human
life. In imaginative writing the words "not only excite
feelings, but they point to the *why* and *wherefore.*
Causes march before them, and consequences follow after them." They are not Hobbesian abstractions but
"links in the chain of the universe, and the grappling-
irons that bind us to it."[9]

Although the style of both poetry and prose makes
similar demands on the imagination, there is an essential difference, which may be traced to the differences in
purpose and subject matter.[10] Hazlitt, of course, is
thinking of the essay rather than prose fiction when he
says that the prose writer aims at "truth, not beauty—
not pleasure, but power."[11] More specifically, he continues, "the man of genius" writing or speaking prose
"can have but one of these two objects; . . . to furnish
us with new ideas, . . . or . . . to rivet our old impressions
more deeply. . . ." In either case, the subject matter,
however "remote or obscure, . . . must be rendered plain
and palpable" in concrete terms.[12] In requiring palpable detail, poetry and prose are alike, but "abstract

truths or profound observations" resist concrete illustration more than "natural objects and mere matters of fact" do.[13] In his search for truthful and convincing expression, the prose writer is both freer and more restricted than the poet. He is free from having to observe the "decorum" of poetry and "all such idle respect to appearances."[14] Specifically Hazlitt applies the word "decorum" to the "balance" he finds lacking in Burke's Windsor Castle metaphor,[15] but judging from his own as well as Burke's practice, he would also allow the prose writer the kind of non-elevating comparisons that he objects to in the metaphysical poets or even the low materials he criticizes in Wordsworth. On the other hand, the prose writer is not as free as the poet to select his own subjects (especially if he is a political writer or a journalist) or to mold his materials into imaginative creations which, although perhaps true to general nature, would not illuminate the specific situation or problem he must deal with. "Invention, not upon an imaginary subject, is a lie. . . ."[16] The prose writer may not allow one "pleasing or striking image" to suggest another, for each image must bear directly on the subject. ". . . nothing can be admitted by way of ornament or relief, that does not add new force or clearness to the original conception."[17]

Burke was the most successful prose writer that Hazlitt knew of. "It has always appeared to me that the most perfect prose-style, the most powerful, the most dazzling, the most daring, that which went the nearest to the verge of poetry, and yet never fell over, was Burke's." In a passage which suggests Burke's own coalescing dilation, Hazlitt compares Burke's style to a chamois rather than an eagle: "it climbs to an almost equal height, touches upon a cloud, overlooks a precipice, is picturesque, sublime—but all the while, instead of soaring through the air, it stands upon a rocky cliff, clambers up by abrupt and intricate ways, and browzes on the roughest bark, or crops the tender flower."[18] Burke's style is "airy, flighty, adventurous," yet it retains its "solidity," never out of sight of its subject, "ris[ing] with the lofty, descend[ing] with the mean, luxuriat[ing] in beauty, gloat[ing] over deformity"—precluded by his materials from "continual beauty" but not from continual "ingenuity, force, originality."[19] Nor from sublimity. Burke achieves—notably in such passages as his comparison of the English Constitution to Windsor Castle—the kind of imaginative aggregation that Hazlitt attributes elsewhere, in almost the same phrasing, to Shakespeare. "Burke most frequently produced an effect by the remoteness and novelty of his combinations, . . . by the striking manner in which the most opposite and unpromising materials were harmoniously blended together. . . ."[20] Despite its elaborateness, Burke's style remains organic. He avoids both the trite affectation of the "florid style" and the set formality of the *"artificial"* style. His thought and feeling determine diction and structure, and are never dissipated by merely "dignified and eloquent" language or by the demands of balance or antithesis. He does not multiply words "for want of ideas, but because there are no words that fully express his ideas, and he tries to do it as well as he can by different ones."[21]

ii

What Hazlitt says of the familiar style in general—and of Burke's style in particular—applies to his own style at its best. He did not, however, learn immediately to render "remote and obscure" ideas "plain and palpable" in concrete language, or to keep his sentences

firm with meaning. In the *Essay* and in his lectures on
philosophy his diction is often abstract and bookish, and
his sentences do not sustain their length. In his metaphysical arguments, he becomes verbose, repetitious, and
tedious, as in an effort to make himself clear he goes over
the same ground time and again. In his early political
writings, however, he saw the need to become more "impressive and vigorous" to combat the "cold, philosophic
indifference" of his time.[22] As a result there are passages,
standing out from labored exposition reminiscent of the
Essay, that are rhetorically elaborate and others that are
incisively simple. Some of his sentences exfoliate with
picturesque images and melodramatic metaphor, along
with emphatic rhythms, elaborate parallelism, and occasional alliteration. One of the opening sentences of
Free Thoughts on Public Affairs pounds home Hazlitt's
idea of patriotism.

It has been called patriotism, to flatter those in power at the ex-
pence of the people; to sail with the stream; to make a popular
prejudice the stalking-horse of ambition, to mislead first and then
betray; to enrich yourself out of the public treasure; to strengthen
your influence by pursuing such measures as give to the richest
members of the community an opportunity of becoming richer,
and to laugh at the waste of blood and the general misery which
they occasion; to defend every act of a party, and to treat all those
as enemies of their country who do not think the pride of a min-
ister and the avarice of a few of his creatures of more consequence
than the safety and happiness of a free, brave, industrious, and
honest people; to strike at the liberty of other countries, and
through them at your own; to change the maxims of a state, to
degrade its spirit, to insult its feelings, and tear from it its well-
earned and proudest distinctions; to soothe the follies of a multitude, to lull them in their sleep, to goad them on in their madness,
and, under the terror of imaginary evils, to cheat them of their
best privileges; to blow the blast of war for a livelihood in journals
and pamphlets, and by spreading abroad incessantly a spirit of defiance, animosity, suspicion, distrust, and the most galling contempt, to make it impossible that we should ever remain at peace

or in safety, while insults and general obloquy have a tendency to provoke those passions in others which they are intended to excite.[23]

Hazlitt's polemical "impressiveness," in a fashion of the day in which Hazlitt soon excelled, also led to personal abuse and ridicule. He would have preferred to attack Malthus' theories "without attacking the author. . . . But the thing was impossible." *The Essay on Population,* therefore, becomes "a miserable reptile performance" disguising "the little, low, rankling malice of a parish-beadle, or the overseer of a workhouse . . . in the garb of philosophy." Malthus seems never to have heard of other passions that disturb society. "But the women are *the devil.*" In his satirical passages, Hazlitt's language becomes plain, and the rhythm conversational. ". . . he must be a strange sawney who could turn back at the church-door after bringing a pretty rosy girl to hear a lecture on the principle of population. . . ."[24] Thus in the midst of tortuous and wearisome restatements of Hazlitt's "refutation" of Malthus, there are swift passages that look forward to the *Letter to William Gifford* and *A Reply to 'Z'*.

As Hazlitt learned to write more imaginatively, the labored exposition of abstract ideas disappeared from his work and he brought all his "impressive" devices under control. As might be expected of someone devoted to the drama, Hazlitt also learned to make good use of narration and dialog. He is capable of short passages of swift and economical narrative, but, as in "The Fight," such passages are interrupted with "reflections" in the manner of his *Table-Talk*.[25] In his later metaphysical essays—such as "Self-Love and Benevolence"—he uses dialog to attain an economy and precision lacking in his earlier discussions of these matters. This dialog, which is weighted with some pretty long speeches, is only superficially dramatic; and its success, as intended, is as a means of communicating ideas and not of illuminating character or advancing action.[26] However, Hazlitt frequently assimilates dialog as well as narrative into the structure of his more imaginative essays. He uses these devices, along with others, to convey the intricate pattern of moods and thoughts that his imagination leads him into.

Hazlitt describes his method as the opposite of "systematic and scientific. . . . Supposing the reader in possession of what is already known, [an author] supplies deficiencies, fills up certain blanks, and quits the beaten road in search of new tracts of observation or sources of feeling."[27] It is a method—unsustained by narrative or logical progression—that puts a great demand on the emotional resources of language to keep the parts in tension. Hazlitt, of course, has abundant resources of this kind. What he says of Burke applies equally well to his own style: he "makes use of the most common or scientific terms, of the longest or shortest sentences, of the plainest and most downright, or of the most figurative modes of speech. He gives for the most part loose reins to his imagination, and follows it as far as the language will carry him."[28] Hazlitt's essays are rich with images, metaphors, and—less often—similes. Unhampered by the decorous restrictions that he placed on the poets of paradox, Hazlitt ranges widely for sense impressions to mold into a reflection of his thought and feeling. Hazlitt's images and figures bear directly on his subject; they are integral with thought and feeling. As Hazlitt and Coleridge walk back to Shrewsbury, the Welsh mountains in the distance are charged with Hazlitt's delight: "As . . . I eyed their blue tops seen through the wintry branches, or the red rustling leaves of the sturdy oak-trees by the road-side, a sound was in my ears as of a Siren's song.

. . ."²⁹ Sometimes, as often noted, an image recreates Hazlitt's experience with a poem or a painting; or it may illustrate his own technique as a painter: "Beneath the shrivelled yellow parchment look of the skin, there was here and there a streak of blood-colour tinging the face; this I made a point of conveying. . . ."³⁰

Hazlitt's aggregated images and metaphors frequently attain the diversity and topographical sweep that he considered essential to sublimity. Hazlitt is fond of using a metaphor or pair of metaphors to characterize a person or thing and then elaborating each metaphor, sometimes in literal language but more often in a complex of additional metaphors or similes. Irish eloquence is "all fire"; Scotch eloquence is "all ice." Byron's verse "glows like a flame"; Scott's "glides like a river."³¹ The elaborating figures usually burst impatiently through the confines of the original comparison. The chamois figure used to describe Burke's style is an exception.³² More typical is Hazlitt's description of Byron: "He is like a solitary peak, all access to which is cut off not more by elevation than distance. He is seated on a lofty eminence, 'cloud-capt,' or reflecting the last rays of setting suns; and in his poetical moods, reminds us of the fabled Titans, retired to a ridgy steep, playing on their Pan's-pipes, and taking up ordinary men and things in their hands with haughty indifference. He raises his subject to himself, or tramples on it; he neither stoops to, nor loses himself in it. . . . Nature must come to him to sit for her picture. . . ."³³ The power of Hazlitt's metaphors most often resides in their pungency, their individual force, in their swift abundance and variety, rather than in a close texture of association either between the things compared in each metaphor or in a series of metaphors. Partly because of the rapid shifting from image to image in a long series and partly because of the diversity of the images themselves, they often do not attain that "indissoluble coalescence" through mutual modification that Hazlitt praises in the great poets and in Burke. The images are charged with enough feeling but not always with highly congruent associations. Sir Walter Scott "strewed the slime of rankling malice and mercenary scorn over the bud and promise of genius, because it was not fostered in the hot-bed of corruption, or warped by the trammels of servility" and so on, for a closely printed page.[34] It would be difficult to supply the equivalent of Antony's "black vesper's pageants"[35] to reduce all this multeity to unity. But in prose, Hazlitt would have said, it is more important to "lay open the naked truth" by making every image bear on the subject.[36] At other times, in the best Romantic tradition of the imagination, an image will reduce a whole essay to concrete oneness. ". . . Milton's *Eve* is all of ivory and gold," says Hazlitt, epitomizing not only his idea of Eve but his analysis of epic poetry.[37] More elaborately, a central image unifies "On the Fear of Death." Looking at a dead child, the writer "could not bear the coffin-lid to be closed—it almost stifled me; and still as the nettles wave in a corner of the churchyard over his little grave, the welcome breeze helps to refresh me and ease the tightness at my breast!" The stifling identification with the dead is dispelled by waving nettles and their suggestion of life's "just value."[38]

iii

Hazlitt also wrote a dry, plain style which gets its effects not from image or metaphor but from terseness or irony, with or without the support of syntactic balance. In the opening sentence of his *Letter to William Gifford* (1819), the direct conversational tone enforces Hazlitt's scorn: "Sir,—You have an ugly trick of saying what is not true of any one you do not like; and it will be the object of this letter to cure you of it."[39] Burke could also flay an opponent, but here the direct insult, the casual despising tone, the easy but malignant assumption of superiority, are more in the manner of Junius.[40] Hazlitt concludes his portrait of Gifford in *The Spirit of the Age* with a double antithesis that once again recalls Junius: "But as Mr. Gifford assumes a right to say what he pleases of others—they may be allowed to speak the truth of him!"[41]

Another clear influence on Hazlitt's curt style, after 1823, is La Rochefoucauld.[42] "I was so struck," Hazlitt writes in his *Characteristics: in the Manner of Rochefoucault's Maxims* (1823), "with the force and beauty of the style and manner, that I felt an earnest ambition to embody some occasional thoughts of my own in the same form. This was much easier than to retain an equal degree of spirit."[43] Hazlitt had difficulty in retaining "an equal degree of spirit" because his imagination frequently got the better of his wit. The aphorism, as La Rochefoucauld uses it, exploits some sort of paradox—not the extreme sort of illogicality or idiosyncrasy that Hazlitt usually calls by that name, but an apparent contradiction which nevertheless strikes the reader as true to much of his experience. It is this contradiction, pointed up by repetition and parallelism, which holds the parts of the aphorism in tension and gives it solidity. Hazlitt sometimes achieves in La Rochefoucauld's manner—"He will never have true friends who is afraid of making enemies"—as well as his cynicism—"We as often repent the good we have done as the ill"[44]—but Hazlitt's aphorisms lack the sustained detachment, as well as the polish, of his models. The differences from La Rochefoucauld are in keeping with what we know of Hazlitt's habit of writing with little polishing or revision, and also with his play of imagination. In La Rochefoucauld the contradiction that binds together the parts of an aphorism usually lies between a commonplace, bland assumption of human virtue and the corrosive evidence of self-love.[45] This loosening of the affections is the method of wit, which Hazlitt admired for its truth (of a sort) and texture,[46] but which he himself could not often sustain. Hazlitt occasionally lets his associations carry him into long aphorisms with specific details.[47] At times the allusions are clearly autobiographical. Numbers 248, 249, 251, 254 ("The contempt of a wanton for a man who is determined to think her virtuous, is perhaps the strongest of all others")[48] remind us that *Characteristics* and *Liber Amoris* were published the same year. Hazlitt, it has been said apropos of his aphorisms, was "bitter and sardonic; and he hated rather than loved his fellow human beings."[49] This statement is not supported either by the *Characteristics* or by Hazlitt's other essays. Many of Hazlitt's aphorisms level their accusations at only part of mankind or suggest at least as much good in human nature as bad.[50] Whereas La Rochefoucauld's aphorisms, in general, are short, detached, cynical, and abstract, Hazlitt's more frequently incline to length, involvement, sympathy, and particulars. His most effective use of the aphorism is probably in combination with his richer style, as in the *Table-Talk* essays, where his occasional short, pointed utterances provide force, variety, unity, and conclusiveness.

iv

Despite his frequent use of parallelism of one sort or another, the structure of Hazlitt's sentences, paragraphs, and essays usually suggests organic growth rather than formal planning—the spontaneous flow of association rather than the exact calculations of reason to which

Hazlitt objected so strenuously in Dr. Johnson's style.[51] His sentences often include symmetrical parts in an unbalanced overall pattern. He frequently pairs adjectives and prepositional phrases,[52] or accumulates sentence members—most often substantives, but very frequently adjectives or prepositional phrases—in threes, fours, or longer series, but especially (and here, once again, he is like Burke) in threes: "The poet of nature is one who, from the elements of beauty, of power, and of passion in his own breast, sympathizes with whatever is beautiful, and grand, and impassioned in nature. . . ."[53] In Burke's triads, it has been pointed out, the third member sometimes seems merely an addition to the sound rather than the sense;[54] but Hazlitt usually keeps the three parts distinct in meaning. His beauty-power-passion triad—like his thought-feeling-action complex—is deeply rooted in his thinking. Hazlitt's parallelism extends, of course, to predicates and to whole clauses, dependent and independent. His practice of building a paragraph by comparison or contrast furnishes many examples. "Chatham's eloquence was calculated to make men *act;* Burke's was calculated to make them *think.*"[55] Usually even Hazlitt's shorter sentences are less symmetrical. "Chatham could have roused the fury of a multitude, and wielded their physical energy as he pleased: Burke's eloquence carried conviction into the mind of the retired and lonely student, opened the recesses of the human breast, and lighted up the face of nature around him."[56] In his long sentences, Hazlitt is like Burke in varying his parallel elements through length, internal structure, and cadence. "Does not Mr. Owen know that the same scheme, the same principles, the same philosophy of motives and actions, of causes and consequences, of knowledge and virtue, of virtue and happiness, were rife in the year 1793, were noised abroad then, were spo-

ing from thy clay-cold bed) when that sad heart is no longer sad, and that sorrow is dead which thou wert only called into the world to feel!"[64] Howe calls this reference elusive,[65] but like any imaginative writer Hazlitt may be allowed the privilege of speaking dramatically in the first person. The next four paragraphs, which begin matter-of-factly enough, proceed in like fashion, from reasoned analogy to exclamations on the pointlessness of life, from familiar phrases like "up and stirring" to the deeper tones. of "this dim, twilight existence," from third person and first person plural to first person singular. Within this section there is a subordinate movement from past to present: first in the impersonal terms of historic events, then with the young man who never "thinks he shall die," and finally with the speaker himself as he approaches death. The images of futility and waste reinforce the reasoned analogy which Hazlitt started with.[66] Then follows a short summary paragraph, which serves as a fulcrum about which the movement of the essay reverses itself. "I have never seen death but once," the speaker continues, "and that was in an infant."[67] From the description of the dead child, he moves on to other pictures of death and to the generalization that death seems a "ghastly monster" because "we think how we should feel, not how the dead feel." After a quotation from Tucker elaborating this sort of sympathetic identification,[68] Hazlitt proceeds to detail, rather briskly in short sentences, the short-lived anguish of those who survive us. "The pathetic exhortation on country tombstones, 'Grieve not for me, my wife and children dear,' &c. is for the most part speedily followed to the letter."[69] Hazlitt is dry and conversational as he turns from everyday life to history, pausing with some pleasure to note that "the rich and titled" are soon forgotten along with everybody else, and ending with one

of his favorite themes: the decline of feeling and imagination in the present "highly civilised and artificial state
of society." This is what accounts for "the effeminate
clinging to life as such, as a general and abstract idea."
Hazlitt concludes with a curt summary: "The most rational cure after all for the inordinate fear of death is to
set a just value on life."[70]

Few of Hazlitt's essays are so symmetrical, but "On
the Fear of Death" represents the structure of Hazlitt's
later essays in several ways. Even when the basic pattern
is narrative, as in "The Fight" or "My First Acquaintance with Poets," brisk reasonableness may alternate
with deep feeling as Hazlitt shifts from third person or
first person plural to first person singular. Frequently,
at or near the end, there is some kind of reversal, so that
the essay ends dispassionately. Diction and sentences respond to mood, ranging from dry colloquialism to dark
and troubled or warmly throbbing imagery, from curt
aphorisms to winding sentences that keep their firmness
through syntactic structure or powerful images. As in
his early essays Hazlitt goes over the same intellectual
ground time and again, no longer in the abstract language of his metaphysics but with an abundance of detail
and imagery that, with contrapuntal effect, refine and
enrich his thought and feeling.

"The Indian Jugglers" begins with a long third-to-
first-person paragraph which gradually develops an analogy: juggling stands for "mechanical excellence," talent
not genius. Hazlitt begins by admiring the juggler's
skill and goes on to point out that its perfection is quite
different from the "ill-pieced transitions, . . . crooked
reasons, [and] lame conclusions" of his own essays. In a
second comparison, Hazlitt develops his analogy more
explicitly, this time using rope-dancing and painting to
show that the "mechanical performer" has the easier task

of "emulating himself," while the artist must "imitate nature." Hazlitt then restates his comparison again, working now from abstract terms—"talent," "genius," "cleverness," "greatness"—to the concrete details and bringing in still another dimension of greatness: "No man is truly great, who is great only in his life-time." Hazlitt completes his essay with an article he had already published on the "Death of John Cavanaugh," the fives-player (*Examiner,* 7 February 1819). This extended concrete detail is perhaps a lazy addition but, as Hazlitt says, "it is *pat* to [his] purpose." Up to this point the essay has continually contrasted merely physical skill with "genius, imagination, feeling, taste." But Cavanaugh carried his physical skill beyond the merely mechanical to a self-forgetting consummation of power that attained a kind of greatness, still remembered.[71]

"On Living to One's-Self" begins with a statement of contentment. In the second paragraph the mood deepens for three pages, but remains calm throughout another third-to-first-person descent. The next paragraph begins: "This sort of dreaming existence is the best." But Hazlitt's dreaming gets him into a dark and bitter mood as he thinks, contrapuntally, of the woes of love, friendship, and marriage. Then there is a quick return to detachment in a short paragraph (the last but one) followed by a quotation from Bolingbroke's *Reflections on Exile.* "Why Distant Objects Please" begins with three successive sinking sequences (*we* to *I;* third person to *we* to *I;* third person to *I)* dealing respectively with distance in space, distance in time, and remembered "scents, tastes, and sounds," the last of these sequences ending with the speaker's recollection of "a voice . . . charm[ing] the moonlight air with its balmy essence, while the budding leaves trembled to its accents" (another "elusive reference," says Howe) and of a "full organ pealing on the ear." Hazlitt abruptly "descend[s] from this rhapsody to the ground of common sense and plain reasoning" with a three-page quotation from Fearn's *Essay on Consciousness,* before concluding with a long third-to-first-person paragraph showing that proximity affects our acquaintance with people more favorably than our acquaintance with places or things.[72]

The integrity of Hazlitt's essays, it must be admitted, is sometimes marred by his use of quotations. Even though part of his pattern of undulations, the extended quotation with which Hazlitt closes an essay is sometimes prolonged until the essay ends distractingly rather than dispassionately, and suggests that Hazlitt needed a block of words to fill out the sheet. Nor are his frequent short quotations always well integrated. Although these quotations fit suitably into Hazlitt's sentence rhythms, the quotation marks and more especially the printed isolation of complete lines of poetry between the parts of a broken paragraph give them a disturbing prominence. Talfourd defended Hazlitt's use of quotations as a "felicitous" fault, "trailing after it a line of golden associations";[73] but the associations are frequently jarring. Often a quotation comes off better if one does not know the original context. It is all very well to allow Coleridge to see "that which was now a horse" made "indistinct as water is in water," but unfortunately these cloud pictures recall very different circumstances and a distinctly un-Coleridgean type named Antony.[74] The Reverend Mr. Irving is not inappropriately described as "a lusty man to ben an Abbot able," but Hazlitt applies the same quotation to a "tall English yeoman" whom he meets on his way to the Fight.[75] Of course, the associations invoked by Hazlitt's quotations were not always the same in Hazlitt's day as they are now. A hundred years before Professors Lowes and Manly, Hazlitt could more suitably describe the tone of the Gospels as "all . . . conscience and tender heart."[76] And it must be added that Hazlitt may select a quotation which is strikingly appropriate and perfectly in keeping with his purpose and tone, as he does when Malthus' *Essay on Population* reminds him of "the title of the old play, 'All for love, or the world well lost.' "[77] Or, among his many misquotations, the altered line may be more suitable to Hazlitt's purpose than the exact original would have been.[78]

vi

As a prose writer Hazlitt may have been guided by the principle of "truth, not beauty—not pleasure, but power"; but when he is at his best—which is often—he attains not only power but a kind of form which gives pleasure. As we have seen, Hazlitt does not make a sharp distinction between truth and beauty (in poetry, they are apparently the same thing) or between poetry and prose. In poetry truth and beauty result from revealing essential (general) qualities in the subject, from discovering order in a variety of objects or events, and from exciting and extending, thereby, the reader's powers of association. Prose does the same thing, but in view of its "practical purpose," the prose writer is less free to use his imagination. His, and the readers', flow of associations must be continually checked by returning to the actual subject. As Hazlitt freed himself, to some extent at least, from the pressure of political writing and dramatic criticism, he freed his imagination at the same time; and in many of his familiar essays it would be difficult to say wherein his subject imposed imaginative limitations different from those of poetry or to say how the pleasure provided thereby differs from the pleasure of what Hazlitt calls truth and beauty.

Hazlitt's essays illustrate the operation of the human

mind which Hazlitt explained in his philosophical works
and on which he based his political ideas as well as his
critical criteria. The mind, he says, is not simply a machine informed and activated by the phenomena of sensation; nor can truth be encompassed in the abstract
propositions of Hobbes' kind of reason. The perception
of truth and the expression of moral values is, on the
contrary, an imaginative and therefore creative process
integrating sensation with thought and feeling. Ideas do
not have an a priori existence but are formed by the creative mind operating on the data of sensation. As a
man's experience accumulates—especially through sympathetic identification with others—he becomes aware of
what is generally true in human life; and when in a state
of association-stimulating emotion, if he is creative
enough, he finds particular means of embodying these
general truths. A work of art or a democratic state thereby becomes an expression of general truth, but more immediately it is a reflection of its creator or creators,
whereby he or they bring various powers—sensation,
thought, feeling, and moral judgment—into dynamic
harmony. Man is naturally free to engage in this creative process, but its consummation may be hindered in
various ways: especially by preconceived ideas (often
imposed by political institutions) or by selfish preoccupation. The self-fulfillment that is one result of the
process is important to both good citizenship and artistic
creation, leading in each case to organic form.

Hazlitt's later essays show this creative process at
work. As he molds his materials to reflect his thoughts
and feelings, his structures show the balance of organic
growth rather than formal planning. He also approaches
a kind of negative capability as he becomes less dogmatic
in asserting his political views and less shrill in voicing
his resentments. He does not exclude the "dark and

doubtful views" of life; in fact, his essays are sometimes a record of their gradual exploration in varied imagery, as in "On the Fear of Death." He does not, of course, achieve the loss of self that results in dramatic form propulsive through a strong unifying action; but he did not pretend to write anything but what he defined as prose. His chief character, like Wordsworth's, remains himself. In his later essays, however, we have a kind of more generalized Hazlitt, whom, despite the pervasive "I," we are ready to accept as a spokesman for more general nature. In fact, the "I" is not invariably easy to identify with the actual Hazlitt and perhaps we should not always try. At times there is still the old anger, of course, and we should not want it lost; if this later Hazlitt has become sympathetic in his treatment of his old enemies, he is no more tolerant of the evils which he thought they represented. He remains as uncompromising as ever in his hatred of fraud, selfish ambition, and tyrannical power.

These essays approach the kind of unity that Hazlitt expected in works of the imagination. As the parts fall into patterns of association, thought and emotion fuse with imagery and rhythm. The essays do not advance like soldiers in close-order drill (which Hazlitt would have detested) but move along like a man out for a walk, who occasionally hurries but who has time to circle through some interesting by-paths. The images emerge crisp and bright or dark and night-blooming. The sentences often strike like bullets or, to use one of Hazlitt's own figures, coil and thrust like a crested serpent.[79] Hazlitt has charged his materials so highly that, long after he expected his essays to be forgotten, they have not dwindled away to paradox, "common places," or mere fancy. They still engage the reader's imagination in the creation of truth and beauty.

References

I

1. *The Complete Works of William Hazlitt,* ed. P. P. Howe (London, 1930-1934), II, 113. (Unless otherwise noted, all references to Hazlitt's writings will be to this edition, and will be designated hereafter simply by the volume and page numbers in Arabic numerals, i. e., 2. 113.)

2. See W. J. Bate, *From Classic to Romantic* (Cambridge, Mass., 1946) and *Criticism: The Major Texts* (New York, 1952); Leo Strauss, *Natural Right and History* (Chicago, 1953); Rosemond Tuve, *Elizabethan and Metaphysical Imagery* (Chicago, 1947); and E. L. Tuveson, *The Imagination as a Means of Grace* (Berkeley, 1960), to all of whom I am indebted in the following pages.

3. Thomas Hobbes, *Leviathan,* ed. M. Oakeshott (Oxford, 1957), pp. 7-8.

4. *Ibid.,* pp. 32, 84-105, 109-113, *et passim.*

5. John Locke, *Essay Concerning Human Understanding,* II, xx, 2; II, xxi, 43; II, xxviii, 5.

6. *Essay Concerning Human Understanding,* II, xxviii, 8, 10; IV, xviii, 8; and the edition ed. A. C. Fraser (Oxford, 1894), Vol. II, p. 477 n.

7. David Hartley, *Observations on Man, His Frame, His Duty, and His Expectations,* 4th ed. (London, 1801), I, 498-501.

8. [Francis Hutcheson], *An Inquiry into the Original of Our Ideas of Beauty and Virtue,* 2d ed. (London, 1726), pp. 11, 111-112, 134-135; *Spectator,* Nos. 411, 413, 419, 420, 421, 580; Hartley, I, ii-iii; II, 244-245; Adam Smith, *The Theory of Moral Sentiments,* 2d ed. (London, 1761), pp. 2-3, 28-31; Dugald Stewart, *Elements of the Philosophy of the Human Mind* (London, 1792), p. 502. See also Anthony [Ashley Cooper, Third] Earl of Shaftesbury, *Characteristicks of Men, Manners, Opinions, Times,* 4th ed. (1727), II, 28-29, 42-43, 414-415, *et passim;* Bate, pp. 43-45; and Tuveson, pp. 47-55, 92-139; 157-163, *et passim.*

9. S. T. Coleridge, *Aids to Reflection,* in *Complete Works,* ed. W. G. T. Shedd (New York, 1878), I, 246. In this paragraph I am indebted to Tuveson, especially chap. I; Northrop Frye, "The Drunken Boat: the Revolutionary Element in Romanticism," in *Romanticism Reconsidered,* ed. N. Frye (New York, 1963), pp. 3-11, *et passim;* Basil Willey, *The Seventeenth Century Background* (New York, 1950), pp. 296-298; M. H. Abrams, *The Mirror and the Lamp* (New York, 1953), especially pp. 21-26, 47-69.

10. 12. 223-224. See also P. P. Howe, *The Life of William Hazlitt* (London, 1947), pp. 19-20; and Herschel Baker, *William Hazlitt* (Cambridge, Mass., 1962), p. 122.

11. 1. 128-129; 16. 122-124. See also 2. 153; 4. 171-172; 5. 166; 11. 30;

16. 76, 118; 19. 34; 20. 12-36; Elisabeth Schneider, *The Aesthetics of William Hazlitt* (Philadelphia, 1933), pp. 14-15, 27-36. See also G. W. Allport, *Becoming* (New Haven, 1955), pp. 7-16.

12. 12. 224; Howe, p. 19; Baker, pp. 27-29, 122; H. W. Stephenson, *William Hazlitt and the Hackney College* (London, 1930), pp. 38, 51-52.

13. 2. 113. Closely paralleling a similar list in the *Proposals* (2. 116-119) is Hazlitt's outline, in the *Lectures*, of "the leading princi₁.les" of the modern philosophy to which he objects (2. 144-145):

"1. That all our ideas are derived from external objects, by means of the senses alone.

"2. That as nothing exists out of the mind but matter and motion, so it is itself with all its operations nothing but matter and motion.

"3. That thoughts are single, or that we can think of only one object at a time. In other words, that there is no comprehensive power or faculty of understanding in the mind.

"4. That we have no general or abstract ideas.

"5. That the only principle of connexion between one thought and another is association, or their previous connexion in sense.

"6. That reason and understanding depend entirely on the mechanism of language.

"7. and 8. That the sense of pleasure and pain is the sole spring of action, and self-interest the source of all our affections.

"9. That the mind acts from a mechanical or physical necessity, over which it has no controul, and consequently is not a moral or accountable agent.—The manner of stating and reasoning upon this point is the only circumstance of importance in which modern writers differ from Hobbes.

"10. That there is no difference in the natural capacities of men, the mind being originally passive to all impressions alike, and becoming whatever it is from circumstances."

14. 2. 114-115.

15. 2. 114, 163, 165-166. See also 1. 19 n.; 5. 296, 347; 6. 132; 12. 44-45, 150-151; 13. 51 n.; 18. 8; 20. 74, 228. Cf. Abraham Tucker, *The Light of Nature Pursued,* 2d ed. (London, 1805), I, 330; ". . . I can see no more reason to suppose one faculty for apprehending, another for judging, and another for reasoning, than to suppose one faculty for seeing blue, another for yellow, and another for scarlet." Hazlitt published an abridgment of Tucker in 1807.

16. 2. 126. See also 2. 137.

17. 2. 146, 147, 158, 162, *et passim.*

18. 2. 146, 147. See *An Essay Concerning Human Understanding,* II, i, 2.

19. *Essay Concerning Human Understanding,* II, ii-xii. While Locke sometimes treats ideas of relations as *coördinate* with complex ideas, in other passages he treats them as *subordinate* (see II, xii, 1, 3, 7). This is the sort of inconsistency that Hazlitt finds fault with. See also Tuveson, pp. 18-22.

20. 2. 149-151.

21. 2. 151-153. See also 2. 213, 280; 12. 150-151. Cf. *Essay Concerning Human Understanding*, II, xii, xiii.

22. 2. 196. See also 2. 138.

23. *Leviathan*, pp. 7-9, 19, 25-26, 53.

24. *Essay Concerning Human Understanding*, III, iii, 6, 11 (quoted, in part, 2. 279). See also II, xxxii; IV, iv.

25. In his *Diversions of Purley* Horne Tooke had argued that there are no abstract or complex ideas but only particular ones, from which abstractions are derived through "contrivances of language" rather than the "imagined *operation of the mind*" (῎Επεα πτεροεντα, or, *The Diversions of Purley*, London, 1805, II, 396; quoted 2. 271). The linguistic contrivance that Tooke—with many mistaken etymologies and an eager proneness to the etymological fallacy—applies to all abstract ideas is their derivation from past participles. Even if we overlook Tooke's philological shortcomings, we must join Hazlitt in wondering how this process excludes any operation of the mind (2. 272).

26. This is the same point that S. I. Hayakawa, with his "Abstraction Ladder," has made available to all freshman English teachers (*Language in Thought and Action*, New York, 1949, pp. 168-170).

27. 2. 204. See also 2. 209, 215, 282, *et passim*.

28. 2. 209-211. See also 1. 124; 2. 191; 20. 10.

29. *Discours sur l'origine de l'inégalité*, in *Œuvres complètes* (Paris, 1865), I, 95: "Toute idée générale est purement intellectuelle; pour peu que l'imagination s'en mêle, l'idée devient aussitôt particulière."

30. 2. 212-213. See also 2. 199-201, and "Introduction" (paragraph 16), *A Treatise Concerning the Principles of Human Knowledge*, in *The Works of George Berkeley*, ed. A. A. Luce and T. E. Jessop (London, 1949), II, 34-35.

31. 2. 210, 215.

32. 2. 209; 12. 46.

33. *Principles of Human Knowledge* (I, 14) and *Three Dialogues*, in *The Works of George Berkeley*, II, 46-47, 178-179, 184-187; David Hume, *A Treatise of Human Nature*, ed. L. A. Selby-Bigge (Oxford, 1896), p. 226 (Part IV, section iv).

34. 2. 180-181. His ideas of truth and reality were not much affected by his recognition that "the relations of the things themselves as they exist separately and by themselves must . . . be very different from their relations as perceived by the mind where they have an immediate communication with each other" (1. 71-72). See also 1. 124 and Schneider, pp. 19-20. Cf. Thomas Reid, *Inquiry into the Human Mind* (vii, 4), in *Works*, ed. W. Hamilton (Edinburgh, 1863), I, 209, *et passim*.

35. *Leviathan*, pp. 13-17, 25-27, 68-69. See also *English Works of Thomas Hobbes*, ed. W. Molesworth (London, 1839), I, xiii.

36. *Leviathan*, pp. xx, 84-85, 93-105, 112, *et passim*.

37. *Of Civil Government* (Everyman's Library, 1924), pp. 61, 120, 180, *et passim*. See also Strauss, pp. 221-229.

38. *Leviathan*, pp. 137-138. See also *English Works*, IV, 273-274, 277-278. Cf. 2. 249.

39. Hartley, I, 501.

40. *Leviathan*, pp. 13-17, 31-39. Hobbes divides pleasures into those

of sense and those of the mind, and displeasures into those of sense, "called pain," and those in "the expectation of consequences, . . . called grief" (p. 34).

41. Hartley, I, 56, 59-61. See also I, 11-12.

42. *Ibid.*, pp. 66, 68-69, 74-75. In his condensation of Hartley, Priestley supplies the following illustration: "The first rudiments of the ideas of *right, wrong,* and *obligation,* seem to be acquired by a child when he finds himself checked and controuled by a superior power. At first he feels nothing but mere *force,* and consequently he has no idea of any kind of restraint but that of mere *necessity.* He finds he cannot have his will, and therefore he submits. Afterwards he attends to many circumstances which distinguish the authority of a *father,* or of a *master,* from that of other persons. Ideas of *reverence, love, esteem* and *dependence,* accompany those commands; and by degrees he experiences the peculiar *advantages* of filial subjection. He sees also that all his companions, who are noticed and admired by others, obey their parents, and that those who are of a refractory disposition are universally disliked.

"These and other circumstances, now begin to alter and *modify* the idea of mere *necessity,* till by degrees he considers the commands of a parent as something that *must not* be resisted or disputed, even though he has a power of doing it; and all these ideas coalescing form the ideas of *moral right,* and *moral obligation,* which are easily transferred from the commands of a parent to those of a magistrate, of God, and of conscience" (Joseph Priestley, *Hartley's Theory of the Human Mind,* London, 1775, pp. xlii-xliii).

43. Hartley, I, 85-86.

44. *Ibid.*, pp. 103-104. See above, pp. 69-70.

45. See Joseph Priestley, *Hartley's Theory of the Human Mind,* pp. xxviii-xxix. Hazlitt probably knew this condensation (see Baker, p. 149), but his quotations are from Hartley unabridged. Cf. 1. 58 and Hartley, I, 69.

46. Hartley, I, 498.

47. 1. 55, 67. Coleridge also rejected Hartley's "corpuscular hypotheses" while accepting the rest of Hartley's volume I (Letter to Godwin dated 4 June 1803, *Collected Letters of Samuel Taylor Coleridge,* ed. Earl Leslie Griggs, Oxford, 1956, II, 949. Quoted in Howe, p. 64). In 1814 Hazlitt expressed his admiration of John Fearn's *Essay on Human Consciousness,* London, 1811 (20. 30 n. See also 8. 63-64, 260-262). Fearn replied to Hartley by arguing that association proceeds not from vibrations but from *"mental Interests"*—that is, from pleasure and pain. "Mental *Association cannot be* an *accident of Matter,"* because pleasure and pain can exist only "in a *sensitive Being.*" The intensity and permanence of these feelings does not depend on the degree of motion that incites them but on something (quite apart from the mind's *"physical character"*) which Fearn calls its *"conscious character"* or "the *Feeling* capacity of *Mind"* (pp. 170, 229-231).

48. 1. 80. My italics.

49. 1. 4, 10, 19 n., 23. See also 1. 11, 21, *et passim.*

50. 1. 79-82.

51. I, 324-367, 504-507.
52. *English Works,* IV, 255. Quoted 2. 252.
53. 2. 253.
54. 2. 246. See also 2. 266; 20. 82.
55. 2. 255, 256, 259.
56. "The Questions Concerning Liberty, Necessity, and Chance," *English Works,* V, 54. Quoted 2. 254. Cf. *English Works,* IV, 240; V, 5, 51.
57. 2. 255.
58. 1. 1, 32, 38. See also 1. 7, 9-10. Hazlitt often repeated these arguments from the *Essay.* See especially his lecture "On Self-Love," 2. 215-244, and "Self-Love and Benevolence" (1828), 20. 162-186.
59. 1. 12, 78. See also 1. 12. Cf. Hartley, I, 498.
60. 1. 80-82. See Adam Smith, *The Theory of Moral Sentiments,* 2d ed. (London, 1761), pp. 2-3.
61. 1. 12-13.
62. 1. 13-16.
63. *Observations on Man,* I, iii, 383.
64. *Ibid.,* II, 244-245; I, ii-iii. See also I, 383 ff.
65. 2. 219.
66. 2. 223. See Hobbes, *Human Nature* (chap. ix, section 10), in *English Works,* IV, 44-45; and *De l'homme,* in *Œuvres complètes d'Helvétius* (Paris, 1818), II, 300: "Mon attendrissement pour les douleurs d'un infortuné est toujours proportionné à la crainte que j'ai d'être affligé des mêmes douleurs."
67. 2. 224-225. See also 17. 121; 20. 45; and *The Works of Joseph Butler,* ed. W. E. Gladstone (Oxford, 1896), II, 36-37 n., 96 n. (Notes to sermons "Upon Human Nature" and "Upon Compassion").
68. 1. 87, 91.
69. 1. 83-84.
70. Fritz Heider, *The Psychology of Interpersonal Relations* (New York, 1958), pp. 4-10, 219, 232-233, 295, *et passim.* See also S. E. Asch, *Social Psychology* (New York, 1952), pp. 354-355; E. Westermarck, *Ethical Relativity* (New York, 1932), pp. 92-94.
71. See Westermarck, pp. 179-182.
72. 11. 102.
73. 9. 51; 17. 312. See also 1. 130-134; 2. 215-245; 20. 162-186; Baker, pp. 140-142, and Howe, *Life,* p. 45.
74. Stewart, *Elements of the Philosophy of the Human Mind,* p. 502. Cf. Johnson, *Rambler,* No. 60. See also W. J. Bate, "The Sympathetic Imagination in Eighteenth Century Criticism," *ELH,* XII (1945), 144-164.
75. Adam Smith, *Theory of Moral Sentiments,* pp. 1-10, 28-31.
76. Hume, *Treatise of Human Nature,* pp. 369-370 (II, vi); [Henry Home, Lord Kames], *Elements of Criticism,* 6th ed. (Edinburgh, 1785), I, 97-98; Joseph Priestley, *The Rudiments of English Grammar . . . and Lectures on Oratory and Criticism* (London, 1826), pp. 314-315. See Leonard M. Trawick III, "Sources of Hazlitt's 'Metaphysical Discovery,'" *PQ,* XLII (1963), 277-282; Roy E. Cain, "David Hume and Adam Smith as Sources of the Concept of Sympathy in Hazlitt," *Papers on English Language and Literature,* I (1965), 133-140.

77. 1. 9. See also 1. 12, 14-15, 21-22, 43, 81.
78. 1. 19 n., 21.
79. 1. 20, 26-27.
80. 1. 26-27, 24-26 n.

II

1. Howe, *Life,* pp. 28-39. Parts of this chapter dealing with Malthus and Godwin appeared originally in my monograph *William Hazlitt and the Malthusian Controversy* (Albuquerque, 1950) and in my articles "Hazlitt and Malthus," *Modern Language Notes,* LX (1945), 215-226, and "Hazlitt's *Principles of Human Action* and the Improvement of Society," in *If by Your Art,* ed. A. L. Starrett (Pittsburgh, 1948), pp. 174-190. These excerpts are reprinted by permission of, respectively, the University of New Mexico Press, the Johns Hopkins University Press, and the University of Pittsburgh Press.

2. H. W. Stephenson, *William Hazlitt and the Hackney College* (London, 1930), pp. 2, 5, 8, 18, 29, *et passim.*

3. G. D. H. Cole, *The Life of William Cobbett* (London, 1927), pp. 195-197; Elie Halévy, *A History of the British People in 1815* (New York, 1924), pp. 218, 229, 245-246; J. L. and Barbara Hammond, *The Village Labourer 1760-1832* (London, 1927), pp. 142-143, 153-154; J. L. and Barbara Hammond, *The Town Labourer 1760-1832* (London, 1928), pp. 87-94, 98, 103, 112 ff.; Hansard, *Parliamentary History,* XXXII (1795), 242-554; William Smart, *Economic Annals of the Nineteenth Century* (London, 1910), I, 263-265, 271-276, 442-443, 455, 493, 530, 548-554, 596-598, *et passim;* Graham Wallas, *The Life of Francis Place* (London, 1925), pp. 25-26, *et passim.*

4. 19. 302-303. The *Project* seems to have been completed about 1828 (19. 366-367).

5. *Leviathan,* pp. 94, 109, *et passim.*

6. *The Works of the Right Honourable Edmund Burke* (London, 1887), III, 271-276.

7. *Ibid.,* pp. 308-310, 312-313, 333. See also IV, 169. Cf. *Leviathan,* pp. 80-86, 94, 109.

8. *Works,* IV, 206-207.

9. *Works,* V, 320-321; IV, 163-166.

10. *Works,* V, 189. See also V, 133.

11. *Works,* III, 310.

12. *Correspondence of the Right Honourable Edmund Burke* (London, 1844), III, 214-215.

13. *Works,* III, 333, 346-347, 352-353.

14. *Ibid.,* pp. 352-354. See also pp. 333-335.

15. *Works,* IV, 174-176.

16. See *Works,* III, 433; IV, 173; V, 209-210; VI, 412; *Correspondence,* III, 145.

17. *Works,* VII, 94-95.

18. *Works,* III, 275.

19. *Ibid.,* pp. 310, 313.

20. *Ibid.,* pp. 308-309.

21. *Ibid.,* p. 254. See also IV, 121, 162.

22. *Works,* IV, 164; VI, 320.

23. *Works,* IV, 173, 176. See also IV, 169, 174. The "general will" is of course Rousseau's term. See above, pp. 55-59.

24. *Works,* V, 284.

25. *Works,* IV, 422-423.

26. ". . . as ability is a vigorous and active principle, and as property is sluggish, inert, and timid, it never can be safe from the invasion of ability, unless it be, out of all proportion, predominant in the representation" (*Works,* III, 297-298). Burke cites, with approval, the extension of representation in Parliament to Wales, Chester, and Durham; he urges representation for Ireland, and would have favored representation for America if distance had permitted; but he opposed more extensive efforts to change the electorate or the constitution of the House of Commons—even though almost half of his 400,000 "people" remained disfranchised (*Works,* I, 372-376, 472-473; II, 148-154; III, 481-482; IV, 291-292, 300-304; VII, 91-104).

27. "The Function of Criticism at the Present Time," in *The Complete Prose Works of Matthew Arnold,* ed. R. H. Super (Ann Arbor, 1962), III, 266-268.

28. *Works,* V, 133-169.

29. James Mackintosh, *Vindiciae Gallicae,* 2d ed. corrected (London, 1791), pp. 208-210, 224-228. He would not, along with the French, disfranchise even the unproductive poor (p. 226).

30. *Ibid.,* pp. 66, 107, 116, *et passim.*

31. *Ibid.,* p. 204.

32. *Ibid.,* pp. 207-208.

33. *Ibid.,* pp. 116, 165, 216, 307.

34. *Ibid.,* pp. 216-218.

35. *Memoirs of the Life of the Right Honourable Sir James Mackintosh,* ed. R. J. Mackintosh, 2d ed. (London, 1836), I, 86-94, 125. See also James Mackintosh, *Miscellaneous Works* (New York, 1873), pp. 35, 38 n., 41 43.

36. *Works,* III, 279; V, 133-169.

37. *Vindiciae Gallicae,* pp. 68-69.

38. ll. 100.

39. *Rights of Man,* in *The Complete Writings of Thomas Paine,* ed. Philip S. Foner (New York, 1945), I, 273-275, 357-359, *et passim.*

40. William Godwin, *An Enquiry Concerning Political Justice* (London, 1793), I, 286-290, 343-345, *et passim.* Godwin acknowledges his debt to Hume. (*Ibid.,* p. 296 n.)

41. *Ibid.,* I, 31, 75, 121-122, 346 ff.; II, 830-831, *et passim.*

42. *Ibid.,* I, 110-112.

43. *Enquiry Concerning Political Justice,* 2d ed. corrected (London, 1796), II, 415-416.

44. *Political Justice,* 1st ed., II, 790-792, 823.

45. *Ibid.,* II, 878-893.

46. *Ibid.,* I, 34.

47. *Ibid.,* II, 564-567.

48. "Benevolence," as used by most contemporary writers, seems to

denote an emotion, whereas "virtue" in *Political Justice* apparently involves only reason without emotional impetus. Later, however, in a memorandum intended "to correct certain errors" in *Political Justice,* Godwin acknowledges the need for emotion in directing voluntary actions, and limits the province of reason "to adjusting the comparison between different objects of desire, and investigating the most successful mode of attaining these objects." Virtuous action will spring from "a disposition naturally kind and well-tempered," but it will be regulated by "general utility." (Quoted in Ford K. Brown, *The Life of William Godwin,* London, 1926, pp. 135-136.)

49. Adam Smith, *An Inquiry into the Nature and Causes of the Wealth of Nations,* ed. Edwin Cannan (London, 1904), I, 142-144; Jeremy Bentham, *Observations on the Poor Bill* (London, 1838), pp. 7-8; Burke, *Thoughts and Details on Scarcity,* in *Works,* V, 145-147; William Pitt, in Hansard, *Parliamentary History,* XXXIV (1800), 1428.

50. "The demand for those who live by wages, it is evident, cannot increase but in proportion to the increase of the funds which are destined for the payment of wages" (*The Wealth of Nations,* I, 70-71).

51. Thomas Robert Malthus, *First Essay on Population 1798* (London, 1926), pp. 11-26, 185-206, *et passim.*

52. *Edinburgh Review,* I (1802), 18-24; 24-26; *A Spital Sermon Preached . . . April 15, 1800,* in *The Works of Samuel Parr,* ed. J. Johnstone (London, 1828), II, 593-594; [Samuel] Whitbread, *Substance of a Speech on the Poor Laws* (London, 1807), pp. 6, 54-57, *et passim;* Hansard, *Parliamentary Debates,* VIII (1807), 865-921; XXXIII (1816), 1115; 3rd series, XXV (1834), 220; Arthur Aspinall, *Lord Brougham and the Whig Party* (Manchester, 1927), p. 73.

53. "Malthus on Population," *Quarterly Review,* XVII (1817), 402.

54. Robert Owen, *The Life of Robert Owen by Himself* (New York, 1920), p. 215; G. D. H. Cole, *The Life of Robert Owen,* 2d ed. (London, 1930), pp. 20-30.

55. [Robert Southey], "Malthus's Essay on Population," *Annual Review,* II (1803), 292.

56. Preface to *Laon and Cythna, The Complete Works of Percy Bysshe Shelley,* ed. Roger Ingpen and Walter E. Peck (London, 1926-1930), I, 241-242.

57. Crane Brinton in *The Political Ideas of the English Romanticists* (London, 1926) stresses Hazlitt's "preoccupation . . . with the problem of bringing down the revolutionary philosophy to the level of human nature" (p. 132) and brings out the anti-rationalism with which Hazlitt attacked Malthus and Bentham; but Professor Brinton has not shown the importance that Hazlitt attached to *benevolence,* in opposition to *self-love,* as a factor in improvement.

58. 19. 308-309.

59. Whitbread, pp. 6, 54-57; F. M. Eden, *The State of the Poor,* ed. A. G. L. Rogers (London, 1928), pp. xxxviii-xliv, 230, 240, 252, 285-286, 319, 372, *et passim; The Annual Register,* 1816, Chronicle, pp. 61-62, 66-68, 69-74, *et passim; Weekly Political Register,* American edition, XXX (18 May 1816), 628-640; *Weekly Political Register,* XXXI (3

Aug., 5 Oct., 14 Dec. 1816), 105-106, 320-325, 625-643. For further references, see *William Hazlitt and the Malthusian Controversy*, pp. 28-42.

60. 8. 325-326; 13. ix-x; 17. 316; W. Carew Hazlitt, *Four Generations of a Literary Family* (London, 1897), I, 187-193; T. N. Talfourd, *Critical and Miscellanous Writings* (Philadelphia, 1852), pp. 124-125; Bryan Waller Procter, *An Autobiographical Fragment and Biographical Notes* (London, 1877), p. 124; Howe, *Life*, p. 354; Baker, p. 460. Like *The Memoirs of the Late Thomas Holcroft* (1810), the *Life of Napoleon* represents a regrettable excursion into scholarly research. On the subject of Napoleon, Hazlitt was incapable of objectivity. As history, the *Life* cannot be taken seriously. For the most part, Hazlitt drew on pro-Napoleonic sources; and when he used less friendly authors, he made changes in their testimony to suit his case. Over two-thirds of the book is made up of translation, summary, or paraphrase, often without acknowledging the source. (See the excellent study by Robert E. Robinson, *William Hazlitt's "Life of Napoleon Buonaparte": Its Sources and Characteristics*, Geneva and Paris, 1959.) Undoubtedly in an age that imposed few restraints of any sort on borrowing from printed sources, Hazlitt felt that his case for Napoleon transcended any notions of scholarly precision and documentation. Although Hazlitt in much of the book is still at his best, the *Life* has not fulfilled his hopes for it. It has attracted few readers, and today it would have even fewer if it were not for *Table-Talk*, the *Spirit of the Age*, and other works which Hazlitt thought were ephemeral.

61. 1. 105, 116.

62. 7. 33. See also 13. 46-54, *et passim*.

63. 7. 50. See also N. J. Padelford and G. A. Lincoln, *International Politics* (New York, 1954), pp. 266-273, 285-287; F. S. C. Northrop, *Philosophical Anthropology and Practical Politics* (New York, 1960), pp. 192, 219-222; and Gordon B. Turner, "The Nature of War," *Naval War College Review*, VIII (March 1956), 24-43. (The opinions expressed by Dr. Turner are his own and do not necessarily reflect those of the Navy Department or the Naval War College.)

64. 19. 303-304.

65. 19. 309-310.

66. 19. 304.

67. 19. 316.

68. 19. 304.

69. Burke, *Works*, V, 321.

70. 7. 267.

71. 13. 52; 17. 65.

72. 1. 305, 312-321, 332-333. See *William Hazlitt and the Malthusian Controversy*, pp. 80-84.

73. *The Rights of Man*, p. 359.

74. 1. 114-115.

75. 1. 12; 12. 46.

76. 11. 18-19. See also 7. 103; 19. 159-161.

77. See also 1. 251, 251 n., 305, 332-333; 19. 305.

78. 1. 238, 312, 360.

79. Hazlitt, more clearly than Malthus, correlates the prudential

check with the improvement of society. "Excess" population, translated into a certain amount of privation, is limited at the point where people, responding to the difficulty of providing for a family, refrain from marriage or from sexual intercourse in order to maintain a standard of living. This responsiveness does not depend, as Malthus indicates, only on a "calculation of consequences" but is increased by a greater command of goods, by consequent notions of "comfort and decency," and by "moral causes" such as the "manners," "habits and character" of the people. Therefore, as long as employers control wages, cutting off relief would depress and degrade the poor still further without making them more prudent. On the other hand, extending cultivation would not—as Malthus had led people to believe—encourage overpopulation; since population can increase only in "consequence of greater industry and knowledge," the actual increase "would . . . denote of itself, that the people would be . . . less likely to involve themselves in wilful distress than before." Thus, writing in 1807, Hazlitt anticipated the usual adaptation of Malthus' principle made to explain the rising standard of living that was simultaneous with increasing population during the nineteenth century. (1. 225, 235, 238, 280, 312, 360. See also 1. 208, 231, 281-282, 314-315, 329-333, 339, *et passim;* and *William Hazlitt and the Malthusian Controversy,* pp. 12-13, 104-116.)

80. 11. 21-22.

81. 11. 129. See also 4. 160-164; 11. 47, 127, *et passim.*

82. 1. 181-182. See also 1. 340, 344, 360.

83. 4. 89 n. See also 4. 88-93; 12. 52, 224.

84. *Discours sur l'origine de l'inégalité parmi les hommes,* in *Œuvres complètes de J. J. Rousseau* (Paris, 1865), I, 118-121; *Du Contrat Social,* I, iii, iv, in *Œuvres,* III, 342-344. Rousseau considers democracy to be possible only in small states, and includes all adult males in the legislative branch of the government.

85. *Discours,* pp. 83-84.

86. *Ibid.,* pp. 81, 85, 89-90, 98-100, *et passim.* See also A. O. Lovejoy, "The Supposed Primitivism of Rousseau's *Discourse on Inequality,*" *Essays in the History of Ideas* (New York, 1955), pp. 14-37.

87. The latter is "un sentiment naturel qui porte tout animal a veiller à sa propre conservation, et qui, dirigé dans l'homme par la raison et modifié par la pitié, produit l'humanité et la vertu." On the other hand, "l'amour-propre n'est qu'un sentiment relatif, factice, et né dans la société, qui porte chaque individu à faire plus de cas de soi que de tout autre, qui inspire aux hommes tous les maux qu'ils se font mutuellement . . ." (*Discours,* p. 149 n.).

88. ". . . C'est ainsi que les usurpations des riches, les brigandages des pauvres, les passions effrénées de tous, étouffant la pitié naturelle et la voix encore de la justice, rendirent les hommes avares, ambitieux et méchans" (*Discours,* pp. 110-111, 113-116).

89. *Discours,* p. 110; Lovejoy, p. 30.

90. *Discours,* p. 110.

91. *De l'Économie politique,* in *Œuvres,* III, 286.

92. *Ibid.,* pp. 281-282.

93. *Ibid.*, pp. 285, 287-288, 293; *Contrat Social*, I, viii; II, i-iii, vii; III, iv; IV, vi; in *Œuvres*, III, 315-316, 318-321, 327-329, 343-344, 382-389. See also Strauss, p. 280.

94. 7. 268.

95. 1. 181-182, 340, 344, 360; 4. 160-162; 11. 6-15, 127-129. Obviously Hazlitt's chronology for the diminution of compassion and the growth of self-love does not correspond to Rousseau's.

96. 13. 40.

97. 7. 267, 273. See also 7. 270; 8. 98; and Burke, *Works*, III, 333.

98. 7. 260, 269, 272.

99. 7. 268-269. See also 7. 272.

100. ". . . L'impulsion du seul appétit est esclavage, et l'obéissance à la loi qu'on s'est precrite est liberté" (*Contrat social*, I, viii, in *Œuvres*, III, 316; *De l'Economie politique*, p. 283).

101. "Ce n'est donc pas tant l'entendement qui fait parmi les animaux la distinction specifique de l'homme que sa qualité d'agent libre" (*Discours*, p. 90).

102. See above, pp. 19-21.

103. 7. 267.

104. 11. [2].

105. 11. 16. See also 11. 37, 44, 56, 66, 86, 127, 157, 178, *et passim*.

106. "The Function of Criticism at the Present Time," in *The Complete Prose Works of Matthew Arnold*, III, 263-264.

107. 11. 8, 37, 47, 100, *et passim*.

108. 11. 38, 39.

109. 11. 37. See also 11. 129.

110. 11. 37.

111. 11. 127-129. See also 11. 37, 44, 66.

112. 11. 145, 80.

113. 11. 65.

III

1. *Henry Crabb Robinson on Books and Their Writers*, ed. Edith J. Morley (London, 1938), I, 153; Baker, pp. 196-197; Howe, *Life*, pp. 159-160.

2. For discussions of the growing contribution of associationist theory to the definition of imagination, see Bate, *From Classic to Romantic*, especially chap. IV, pp. 93-128, and "The Sympathetic Imagination in Eighteenth Century Criticism," *ELH*, XII (1945), 144-164.

3. *Leviathan*, pp. 9-10, 30, 43-44.

4. *An Essay Concerning Human Understanding*, III, x, 34.

5. *Essay on Criticism*, Part I, line 82. See also John Ogilvie, *Philosophical and Critical Observations on the Nature, Character, and Various Species of Composition* (London, 1774), I, 265.

6. "Milton," "Pope," in *Lives of the English Poets*, in *Works*, IX, 160, 167-168, 172-173; XI, 193; *Rambler*, Nos. 4, 89, 125, 134, 208; *Idler*, No. 44; *Rasselas*, chap. 44. See R. D. Havens, "Johnson's Distrust of the Imagination," *ELH*, X (1943), 243-255.

7. William Duff, *An Essay on Original Genius* (London, 1767), pp.

8-9; Alexander Gerard, *An Essay on Genius* (London, 1774), pp. 37-38. Wordsworth, in his 1815 Preface, still finds what he calls judgment necessary "to decide how and where, and in what degree, each of these faculties [Observation and Description, Sensibility, Imagination and Fancy, and Invention] ought to be exerted."

8. See above, pp. 178-179 (note 48).

9. See above, pp. 26-27.

10. *Leviathan*, p. 43; Hartley, I, 383-384; Gerard, pp. 46, 67, 149-154, 161-163, 165-166, *et passim;* Hugh Blair, *Lectures on Rhetoric and Belles Lettres* (London, 1783), II, 312; Ogilvie, I, 355. See also Bate, "The Sympathetic Imagination in Eighteenth Century Criticism," pp. 150-156.

11. *Spectator*, Nos. 412, 413, 414.

12. *Spectator*, Nos. 411, 416, 418.

13. Sir Joshua Reynolds, *Discourses on Art*, ed. R. R. Wark (San Marino, California, 1959), pp. 42, 44, 230, 231, 234. .The entire fifteen discourses were first published together in 1797; they were delivered as lectures 1769-1790.

14. Evidently Hazlitt knew Tucker's work before he completed the *Essay*, for in 1803 Coleridge wrote Godwin, "A friend of mine, every way calculated by his Taste, & prior Studies for such a work is willing to abridge & systematize [*The Light of Nature Pursued*] from 8 to 2 Vol. . . . (letter dated 4 June 1803, *Collected Letters of Samuel Taylor Coleridge*, II, 949; quoted by Howe, *Life*, p. 64). Alexander Gerard also turns over to the imagination some of the functions once belonging to reason. The "discovering and finding out of proofs" and "the regular and methodical disposition of them"—both of which Locke attributed to reason—Gerard gives to the imagination, leaving reason only "perceiving their connection" and "inferring a just conclusion." What imagination has taken over belongs to genius; what reason is left with "implies, not genius, but mere capacity." (*An Essay on Genius*, pp. 33-35.)

15. Abraham Tucker, *The Light of Nature Pursued*, 2d ed. (London, 1805), II, 1-6. See also [Hazlitt's] *An Abridgment of the Light of Nature Pursued* (London, 1807), pp. 81-84.

16. Tucker, II, 16. Cf. Hartley, I, 103-104 (quoted above, p. 18).

17. *Abridgment*, p. 86; Tucker, II, 16-17.

18. Ogilvie, I, 296-302.

19. Blair, II, 372. See also Gerard, pp. 322, 330.

20. *Spectator*, No. 413.

21. [Henry Home, Lord Kames], *Elements of Criticism*, 6th ed. (Edinburgh, 1785), I, 238-239; II, 183, 186; Dugald Stewart, *Elements of the Philosophy of the Human Mind* (London, 1792), p. 494. Both are quoted in Tuveson, *The Imagination as a Means of Grace*, pp. 153-156, 182-183. See also W. K. Wimsatt and C. Brooks, *Literary Criticism: A Short History* (New York, 1957), p. 284.

22. Edmund Burke, *A Philosophical Enquiry into the Origin of our Ideas of the Sublime and Beautiful*, ed. J. T. Boulton (London, 1958), "Introduction on Taste," p. 17. See also *The Idler*, No. 44.

23. *Spectator*, Nos. 414, 416.

24. Gerard, pp. 29-30.

25. *Ibid.*, pp. 30, 163. See also Archibald Alison, *Essays on the Nature and Principles of Taste* (Edinburgh, 1790), pp. 54-55.

26. Gerard, p. 41; Duff, p. 7. See also Tucker, I, 222-227; Hartley, I, 66-72, 74-75, 292, 317; Ogilvie, I, 96, 101-106, 328, *et passim*.

27. *Spectator,* Nos. 160, 291, 592; Reynolds, Discourses I, III, VI, IX, XI, pp. 17, 44, 97-98, 191; Edward Young, *Conjectures on Original Composition,* ed. Edith J. Morley (Manchester, 1918), pp. 6-7, 13-18, 24-25, *et passim.* See also Wimsatt and Brooks, *Literary Criticism,* pp. 286-290.

28. Duff, p. 6. See also Gerard, pp. 27-32; Stewart, I, 497.

29. René Wellek, *A History of Modern Criticism: 1750-1950,* Vol. II, *The Romantic Age* (New Haven, 1955), pp. 188-191.

30. Professor Schneider points out that Hazlitt's analysis of the imagination in the *Essay* "precedes by some years the earliest published remarks on the subject by Wordsworth and Coleridge" (pp. 99-100).

31. 5. 3, 10; 8. 5-9. See also 4. 72-76; 12. 245.

31. George Watson in his *The Literary Critics* (Penguin Books, 1962, pp. 135-139) is unnecessarily querulous about this essay. Especially if "On Poetry in General" is read in the light of eighteenth-century theories of imagination, or merely related to Hazlitt's other essays on the subject, one need not share Mr. Watson's "hopeless confusion" about its meaning. Professor Wellek's treatment of the same questionable passages is better informed and more judicious (p. 200).

33. 5. 3-4; 12. 51. See also 6. 23.

34. On 18 July 1815 Hazlitt wrote to Jeffrey (autograph letter, The Yale University Library) to ask him to make a change in the article on *Sismondi's Literature of the South* which Hazlitt had submitted to the *Edinburgh Review:* "In the beginning of the account of Dante for 'the external image' read 'external appearance.' Imagery the French certainly have not, which the word image would imply. What I mean is that all their ideas are positive & definite or formal." The requested change was not made (16. 41).

35. 5. 3.

36. Quoted 5. 4, from *Cymbeline,* II, ii, 19-20. Hazlitt's quotations are notoriously inaccurate, but in most cases, for my present purpose, it would only be cumbersome to indicate corrections.

37. IV. iv. 1-14, quoted 1. 25 n. I. A. Richards uses the same passage to illustrate *Coleridge on Imagination* (New York, 1950), pp. 93-94.

38. See above, p. 13.

39. 5. 3-4. See also 4. 225-226, 259; 5. 10, 50-51; 7. 51; 12. 45-46, 257; 20. 228; *et passim.*

40. 5. 10-11. See also 4. 271, 12. 245.

41. 8. 42. See also 8. 47; 12. 46, 55, 341; 20. 211.

42. 5. 11-12. See also 5. 61-62; 16. 93-94, 136.

43. 4. 162.

44. 1. 21; 8. 33-36. See also 1. 50-51; 8. 104; 12. 46; 20. 72-73.

45. 8. 40-42. See also 4. 260; 12. 150-151.

46. 8. 42-43.

47. 9. 228; 11. 7. See also 5. 204.

48. 1800 Preface.

49. *Ibid.*

50. 8. 44. See also 20. 387.

51. 1. 13.

52. 20. 369. See also 5. 47-48; 8. 42-43.

53. 5. 53.

54. 8. 9-10.

55. 8. 10. See also 4. 73-74; 8. 14.

56. 5. 204; 8. 9. My italics. See also 8. 122-145; 18. 62-84. Cf. *Rasselas*, chap. 10.

57. Discourse III, p. 47; *The Idler*, No. 82, in *The Works of Sir Joshua Reynolds*, ed. E. Malone (London, 1798), II, 237.

58. 18. 159. See also 5. 204.

59. Discourse III, p. 47.

60. Discourse XI, p. 192.

61. *The Idler*, No. 79, in *Works*, II, 230-231. See also Discourse XI, pp. 192-193.

62. 18. 158-159. See also 8. 14. Professor Schneider suggests the possible influence of Diderot (pp. 56-57). See "Essai sur la peinture" in *Œuvres complètes de Diderot* (Paris, 1876), X, 461.

63. 18. 78-79.

64. Discourse XIII, pp. 230-231. See above, pp. 68-69.

65. 4. 68; 18. 78. See also 20. 387. Cf. Discourse XI, p. 192.

66. *Light of Nature*, II, 149-151; I, 259-262.

67. *Observations on Man*, I, 419.

68. *Light of Nature*, II, 152-155.

69. Alison, pp. 127-133; 5. 139. See also Walter J. Hipple, *The Beautiful, the Sublime, and the Picturesque in Eighteenth-Century British Aesthetic Theory* (Carbondale, 1957), pp. 152-153, 167-168; Samuel H. Monk, *The Sublime: A Study of Critical Theories in XVIII-Century England* (New York, 1935), p. 151; Tuveson, pp. 190-191; Wellek, pp. 114-115. See also Thomas Constable, *Archibald Constable and His Literary Correspondents* (Edinburgh, 1873), II, 217 (cited by Baker, p. 215). For a pertinent discussion of "expression," see Eugene C. Elliott, "Reynolds and Hazlitt," *Journal of Aesthetics and Art Criticism*, XXI (1962), 73-79.

70. See below, chap. V.

71. 4. 75. See also 4. 152; 8. 10.

72. 19. 74.

73. 4. 73-74; 18-20; 8. 10. Cf. Tucker, I, 260-262.

74. *Spectator*, No. 413.

75. See above, pp. 137-138.

76. 1800 Preface. See 5. 53, 5. 69-70, *et passim*.

77. 12. 290; 10. 130; 4. 77-78. My italics.

78. 5. 26-27; 4. 79-80, quoted from *Paradise Lost*, III, 438-439; V, 297.

79. *Light of Nature*, II, 150.

80. 19. 11. See also 12. 54-55. As Miss Schneider points out, Hazlitt's emphasis is generally "upon variety as Coleridge's was upon unity. Yet both recognized the other end of the antithesis . . ." (p. 135). Cf. Home, I, 214-215.

81. 4. 75.

82. See Longinus, *On the Sublime,* sections 8, 9, 39, and especially 35; Tuveson, pp. 102-105.

83. *Spectator,* Nos. 412, 413, 414.

84. *Spectator,* No. 413.

85. *Sublime and Beautiful,* pp. 39, 57-87 (I, vii; II, i-xxii).

86. *Ibid.,* pp. 35-37, 39-40, 51 (I, iv, vii, xviii).

87. *Ibid.,* p. 57 (II, i).

88. *Ibid.,* pp. 40-42, 51, 113-117 (I, viii-x, xviii; III, xiii-xviii).

89. Discourse XV, p. 276.

90. *Idler,* No. 79, in *Works,* II, 230-231; Discourse XV, p. 277; Discourse XIII, pp. 237-238. See Hipple, pp. 142-143.

91. 6. 165-166. See Home, I, 221.

92. 18. 164-165.

93. *Sublime and Beautiful,* p. 95 (III, iii). See also Home, I, 214-215.

94. 4. 68-70.

95. 5. 12, 61-62. Cf. 6. 50.

96. Ogilvie, I, 135. Cf. Home, I, 232.

97. 18. 164.

98. *Sublime and Beautiful,* p. 132 (IV, iii).

99. Alison, p. 42.

100. 6. 23; "Life of Cowley," in *Lives of the English Poets, Works,* IX, 21. See also 8. 145; 11. 9; 12. 341; Alison, pp. 42, 52-53; *Sublime and Beautiful,* pp. 62, 138 (II, iv; IV, x); Monk, pp. 148-150.

101. 11. 9.

102. See Stephenson, *William Hazlitt and the Hackney College,* pp. 50-56; Baker, pp. 29-36.

103. 5. 51. See also 8. 42; 12. 341. Cf. Coleridge, *Biographia Literaria,* chap. xiv: "The poet . . . brings the whole soul of man into activity."

IV

1. Sylvan Barnet, "Bernard Shaw on Tragedy," *PMLA,* LXXI (1956), 893; H. A. Meyers, *Tragedy: A View of Life* (Ithaca, 1956), pp. 166-171; H. J. Muller, *The Spirit of Tragedy* (New York, 1956), pp. 242, 252; R. B. Sewall, *The Vision of Tragedy* (New Haven, 1959), p. 84. This chapter is based largely on materials from three of my previously published articles: "Liberalism and Hazlitt's Tragic View," *College English,* XXIII (1961), 112-118; "Hazlitt's Preference for Tragedy," *PMLA,* LXXI (1956), 1042-1052; "More on Hazlitt's Preference for Tragedy," *PMLA,* LXXIII (1958), 444-445. The first of these is quoted by permission of the National Council of Teachers of English, and the other two by permission of the Modern Language Association.

2. This has frequently been pointed out, but for recent and convincing evidence, see Charles H. Shattuck, *Bulwer and Macready: A Chronicle of the Early Victorian Theatre* (Urbana, 1958).

3. See above, pp. 43-44.

4. Concerning Malthus' principle of population, J. S. Mill wrote: "This great doctrine, originally brought forward as an argument against the indefinite improvability of human affairs, we took up with

ardent zeal in the contrary sense, as indicating the sole means of realizing that improvability by securing full employment at high wages to the whole labouring population through a voluntary restriction of the increase of their numbers" (*Autobiography,* New York, 1944, chap. IV, p. 74).

5. 5. 5.

6. 4. 13.

7. 6. 5-9.

8. 6. 31-32, 35, 37, 154-155 n.

9. 5. 69-70. See Stuart M. Tave, *The Amiable Humorist* (Chicago, 1960), pp. 209-217, 241.

10. 6. 39-41.

11. 6. 154-155 n.

12. The "pursuit of uncertain pleasure and idle gallantry," says Hazlitt, prompts most of the action. "It is the salt of comedy, without which it would be worthless and insipid. It makes Horner decent, and Millamant divine" (6. 14). This seems to be the idea that Lamb, three years later, published in his essay "On the Artificial Comedy of the Last Century" (*The Works of Charles and Mary Lamb,* ed. E. V. Lucas, London, 1903, II, 141-147). Lamb never says that Restoration comedy did not represent real life in the time of Charles II, but what it does represent, he insists, is not to be confused with real life as 19th-century theatre-goers know it. Artificial comedies, therefore, "are a world of themselves almost as much as fairy-land." In this world the only business of the characters is "idle gallantry" or, again, "the undivided pursuit of lawless gallantry," and although the result in the actual world would be moral chaos, "no such effects are produced in *their* world" (pp. 141-144). Because Lamb and Hazlitt knew each other intimately and undoubtedly developed many of their ideas in conversation with each other, the problem of originality can hardly be solved.

13. Matthew Arnold, *Mixed Essays, Irish Essays, and Others* (New York, 1924), p. 440.

14. 5. 46.

15. 5. 58, 5. 61.

16. 4. 110. Cf. A. W. Schlegel, *A Course of Lectures on Dramatic Art and Literature,* tr. J. Black (London, 1846), p. 43. When Black's translation appeared in 1815, Hazlitt reviewed it for the *Edinburgh Review.*

17. 5. 52. Hazlitt's distinction between tragedy and the epic closely parallels Burke's between "Astonishment," which is "the effect of the sublime in its highest degree," and its "inferior effects" of "admiration, reverence, and respect." "Astonishment," says Burke, "is that state of the soul, in which all its motions are suspended, with some degree of horror." Burke does not, however, exclude Milton from the highest sublimity. (*The Sublime and Beautiful,* pp. 57, 59, 61-62, 80 [II, i, iii, iv, xiv].)

18. 8. 42; 5. 51, 57.

19. 5. 51, 60, 64.

20. 4. 153; 12. 55. See also 12. 47-48. Cf. Shelley, "A Defence of Poetry," in *Complete Works,* VII, 121.

21. 4. 200.

22. 5.6.

23. 4. 272.

24. 5. 7.

25. 6. 185.

26. 6. 353; 16. 413, 89. See also 5. 8-10; 6. 182-185, 350-353; 16. 58-59, 64-66, 76, 89-90.

27. *The Sublime and Beautiful,* pp. 39, 46-47 (I, vii, xiv, xv); 5. 5-8. See also S. Barnet and W. P. Albrecht, "More on Hazlitt's Preference for Tragedy," *PMLA,* LXXII (1958), 443-445.

28. *The Sublime and Beautiful,* p. 47 (I, xv).

29. 5. 6-8; 20. 274.

30. Lionel Trilling, *Matthew Arnold* (New York, 1939), p. 376.

31. *Preface to Shakespeare,* in *Works,* II, 91.

32. 16. 6; 4. 154; 5. 6, 268-270.

33. 4. 200. See also 4. 306. Even when the great English tragedies were being written, critics and the poets themselves defended tragedy as revealing God's justice consummated (Clifford Leech, *Shakespeare's Tragedies,* London, 1950, pp. 22-27, *et passim*).

34. 6. 353.

35. 6. 350. Cf. De Quincey, "Theory of Greek Tragedy," *Collected Writings,* ed. D. Masson (London, 1897), X, 342-359, especially 347-350.

36. 16. 61, in a review of A. W. Schlegel's *Lectures on Dramatic Literature.* Especially in the first part of the *Characters of Shakespear's Plays,* Hazlitt frequently depends on Schlegel; but here, as Miss Schneider points out, "He draws the contrast [between the classical and the romantic] far less at the expense of the ancients than does Schlegel, who dwells at some length on the superiority of Christianity. . . . It is consistent with Hazlitt's usual avoidance of the subject of religion in his own works that he here minimizes as far as possible Schlegel's emphasis upon it" (p. 133). See also Baker, pp. 29-36.

37. 4. 171; "Preface to the Works of Shakespear," in *The Works of Alexander Pope,* ed. E. Elwin and W. J. Courthope (London, 1886), X, 535.

38. *De Poetica,* trans. I. Bywater, *The Works of Aristotle,* ed. W. D. Ross (Oxford, 1924), XI, chaps. 2, 13-15.

39. 4. 215.

40. 4. 232, 233, 272-273.

41. 12. 55; 6. 348.

42. 6. 347.

43. 6. 355.

44. 4. 258. See also 4. 191, 192, 197, 204, 217, *et passim*.

45. See also Baker, pp. 305, 308, and above, p. 139.

46. Sidney, *An Apologie for Poetrie,* pp. 30-31; Milton, Preface to *Samson Agonistes; Spectator,* No. 39; Schlegel, *Lectures on Dramatic Art and Literature,* pp. 44-46; Arnold, *Mixed Essays, Irish Essays, and Others,* pp. 440-441; Joseph Wood Krutch, "The Tragic Fallacy," *Atlantic Monthly,* CXLII (1928), 604; Bertrand Russell, *Mysticism and Logic* (New York, 1929), p. 53. Examples could be multiplied, with, of course, something to be said in favor of comedy (e.g., Ben Jonson,

"Timber, or Discoveries," *Critical Essays of the Seventeenth Century*, ed. J. E. Spingarn, Oxford, 1908, I, 55-56).

V

1. 4. 161; 5. 82-83. This chapter, particularly the latter part, includes material from my article "Hazlitt on the Poetry of Wit," *PMLA*, LXXV (1960), 245-250. This is reprinted by permission of the Modern Language Association.

2. 5. 68.

3. See Wellek, *A History of Modern Criticism*, II, 200-205.

4. 5. 69-70. See also 4. 77; 5. 1.

5. Duff, *Essay on Original Genius*, p. 89; Stewart, *Elements of the Philosophy of the Human Mind*, p. 305. See also J. Bullitt and W. J. Bate, "Distinctions between Fancy and Imagination in Eighteenth-Century English Criticism," *MLN*, LX (1945), 8-15, in which Duff and Stewart are quoted; and G. C. Watson, "Contributions to a Dictionary of Critical Terms: *Imagination* and *Fancy*," *Essays in Criticism*, III (1953), 201-214.

6. 6. 248.

7. 5. 150, 152; 8. 255; 9. 243; 11. 170, 173; 16. 413, 414.

8. 5. 20, 36, 44; 11. 170, 173; 16. 413, 414.

9. 6. 23; 5. 73. See also 9. 237-238.

10. 5. 112. See also 5. 14, 6. 51.

11. 5. 35, 88, 151; 6. 53, 72, 249.

12. 8. 255. See also 5. 152; 6. 249; 11. 173; 16. 414.

13. James Beattie, *Dissertations Moral and Critical* (London, 1783), p. 72; Duff, pp. 24, 48-52, 58, 70; Stewart, pp. 305-309; Thomas Cogan, *Ethical Treatise on the Passions* (Bath, 1807), I, 209, 249. All of these books, with other appropriate references, are quoted by Bullitt and Bate.

14. See above, pp. 128, 129, 133.

15. 4. 160-164; 18. 5-10.

16. I am indebted, on this point, to Alice Meyer Linck, "The Psychological Basis of Hazlitt's Criticism" (Unpublished University of Kansas Ph. D. Dissertation, Lawrence, 1960), pp. 121-122.

17. 6. 322-323, 350, *et passim;* 9. 236-245.

18. Coleridge, of course, argues that a poem cannot be all poetry but that all the parts must be in harmony (*Biographia Literaria*, chap. XIV).

19. 6. 51, 57.

20. 6. 51, 54-57; 9. 237, 238.

21. *Leviathan*, p. 43.

22. *Essay Concerning Human Understanding*, III, x, 34. See p. 64 above.

23. *Essays of John Dryden*, ed. W. P. Ker (Oxford, 1900), I, 14, 172, 190; *An Essay on Criticism*, Part II, lines 297-298. ". . . wit," says Richard Blackmore, "is that which imparts Spirit to our Conceptions and Diction, by giving them a lively and novel, and therefore an agreeable Form . . ." (*Essays upon Several Subjects*, London, 1716, I, 92).

24. "Life of Cowley," in *Lives of the English Poets, Works,* IX, 20.

25. *Spectator,* No. 62.

26. 6. 15-17, 23, quoted from *Hudibras,* II, ii, 31-32. See also 20. 360.

27. 6. 24; quoted from *Essay on Criticism,* I, 9-10.

28. 5. 100-101; 19. 74, 78-79.

29. Preface to the Second Edition of the *Lyrical Ballads;* "Essay Third," *On the Principles of Genial Criticism,* in *Felix Farley's Bristol Journal* (Aug. and Sept., 1814), reprinted by J. Shawcross, ed. *Biographia Literaria* (Oxford, 1907), II, 238-242. See also Bate, *From Classic to Romantic,* p. 104.

30. 19. 78-79.

31. 6. 31-32, 35, 37; 154-155 n.

32. 5. 68-72. Cf. Wellek, p. 204.

33. 6. 15, 19, 23-24.

34. C. Brooks and R. P. Warren, *Understanding Poetry,* rev. ed. (New York, 1950), p. 175.

35. 4. 65.

36. 19. 20.

37. 4. 65.

38. 19. 11.

39. 4. 65-66.

40. Wellek, p. 204.

41. 6. 49-51. Thus, as Wellek has pointed out (p. 204), Hazlitt objects to Donne, Cowley, Crashaw, etc., by "expound[ing] the standard neoclassical theory of metaphor," but it is this theory used to express his own preference for intense feeling as a means to truth. With "the logic of the schools, or an oblique or forced construction of dry literal matter-of-fact," these poets obscure "the face of nature" and " the secrets of the heart" (6. 50).

42. 6. 58. Hazlitt is quoting from Cowley's "Hymn, to Light," lines 1-2.

43. 6. 23-24. Cf. Johnson, "Life of Cowley," *Works,* IX, 21.

44. 5. 54. "Doubtless," I. A. Richards has written, "the ideal case of Imagination is rare; if enough of the possibilities of the part-meanings come in we overlook any that must stay out. With Fancy, we either 'overlook' them in quite another sense, we voluntarily and expressly ignore them; or we let an awareness of their *irrelevance* in to gain a mixed effect, of burlesque for instance . . ." (*Coleridge on Imagination,* New York, 1950, p. 92).

45. 5. 54.

46. "Lectures of 1811-12," *Coleridge's Shakespearean Criticism,* ed. T. M. Raysor (Cambridge, Mass., 1930), II, 124. See also Stewart, p. 295, and Bullitt and Bate, p. 13.

47. "Life of Cowley," *Works,* IX, 20.

48. 5. 54. The comparisons quoted by Hazlitt are from *Troilus and Cressida,* I. iii. 227-230; III. iii. 115-123, 222-225.

49. 6. 24. Hazlitt is quoting, with customary inaccuracy, from *Lear,* I, iv.

50. 4. 260. See also 16. 94; 17. 159; 20. 276.

51. 5. 6-8; 4. 271-272; 20. 274.

VI

1. Part of this chapter, which appeared previously as "Hazlitt on Wordsworth; or, the Poetry of Paradox," in *Six Studies in Nineteenth-Century English Literature and Thought,* ed. H. Orel and G. J. Worth (Lawrence, Kansas, 1962), pp. 1-21, is republished by permission of the University of Kansas Humanistic Studies.

2. 19. 15; T. S. Eliot, "The Metaphysical Poets," in *Selected Essays* (New York, 1950), pp. 247-248.

3. 19. 15.

4. 16. 82, 269; 11. 79, 30. See also 11. 37.

5. 19. 15; 18. 302, 306-309. Keats' letters dated 22 Nov. 1817, 27 (?) Dec. 1817, about 27 Oct. 1818, and 19 March 1819, *The Letters of John Keats 1814-1821,* ed. H. E. Rollins (Cambridge, Mass., 1958), I, 184-185, 193-194, 388-390; II, 79-80. See also Lionel Trilling, "Introduction" to *The Selected Letters of John Keats* (Garden City, N.Y., 1956), pp. 27-28; Herschel M. Sikes, "The Poetic Theory and Practice of Keats: The Record of a Debt to Hazlitt," *PQ,* XXXVIII (1959), 401-412.

6. Douglas Bush, "Keats and His Ideas," in *The Major English Romantic Poets: A Symposium in Reappraisal,* ed. C. D. Thorpe, *et al.* (Carbondale, Ill., 1957), pp. 237-238.

7. 5. 6.

8. 11. 64-66. See also Charles I. Patterson, "Hazlitt as a Critic of Prose Fiction," *PMLA,* LXVIII (1953), 1003.

9. 4. 214-215, 7. 142. See also 4. 200, 271-272; 5. 5-8, 347-348.

10. 5. 87, 90.

11. 5. 90, 86. Hazlitt is quoting from *The Seasons,* "Spring," 1-4.

12. On occasion Hazlitt uses personification himself (the timid and imploring daisy, 5. 103) and well-worn epithets (the enamelled bank, etc., 17. 161).

13. 5. 86-87.

14. Hazlitt mentions—without specific detail—the "mechanical and common-place" in Gray's "Ode on a Distant Prospect of Eton College," but he defends—again without details—the diction of the "Elegy in a Country Churchyard" against Wordsworth's criticism that it is "unintelligible." Hazlitt has little to say about archaisms in poetry, but is not favorably impressed by Chatterton's "repetition of a few obsolete words, and . . . mis-spelling of common ones." Regarding Latinisms, Hazlitt's specific objection is to their use in prose, rather than in poetry. (5. 118, 124, 105. See above, pp. 151-152.)

15. 12. 8.

16. 6. 347.

17. 6. 354.

18. 16. 82. See A. W. Schlegel, *A Course of Lectures on Dramatic Art and Literature,* trans. John Black (London, 1846), pp. 265-266. Hazlitt's review is of Black's translation, 1815 edition.

19. 16. 89. Cf. Schlegel, p. 270.

20. 6. 354. See also 12. 55, 16. 89.

21. 16. 90. Cf. Schlegel, p. 267.

22. 16. 89-90. Cf. Schlegel, p. 261.

23. 4. 175. See also 6. 347. Cf. Schlegel, pp. 266-267, 273-274.

24. 6. 357. See also 6. 75, 6. 356. Otway, Hazlitt adds in writing of *Venice Preserved,* "is the only writer of this school, who, in the lapse of a century and a half, has produced a tragedy (upon the classic or regular model) of indisputable excellence and lasting interest. . . . Otway always touched the reader, for he himself had a heart" (6. 354-355). In another essay, however, Hazlitt approves of the objectifying power of Dryden's reason: "Dryden's plays are better than Pope could have written; for though he does not go out of himself by the force of imagination, he goes out of himself in the form of common-places and rhetorical dialogue" (5. 81-82).

25. 6. 359, 347.

26. 6. 360, 362.

27. 5. 161-162; 82-83.

28. 5. 162.

29. Letter dated 7 April 1817, *The Letters of William and Dorothy Wordsworth: The Middle Years,* ed. E. de Selincourt (Oxford, 1937), II, 781; Charles Whibley, "Hazlitt v. Blackwood's Magazine," *Blackwood's Magazine,* CCIV (1918), 388-398.

30. 16. 233.

31. 19. 11; Wellek, p. 210; *Critical and Miscellaneous Writings of T. Noon Talfourd,* p. 129 (from *The Examiner,* 14 and 21 Oct. and 4 Nov. 1832, pp. 661-662, 678, 708-709). See also T. N. Talfourd, *Memoirs of Charles Lamb* (London, 1892), p. 180.

32. 11. 80; 16. 267; 8. 255; 11. 77, 71; 16. 242, 240. See also 4. 13, 76 n.; 16. 265; 18. 305.

33. 19. 18.

24. 19. 18-19.

35. 19. 15-16; Willey, *The Seventeenth Century Background,* pp. 296-297.

36. 19. 13-14; 12. 59-60.

37. 11.89. See also 8. 44.

38. 4. 250-251; 19. 33-35.

39. 11. 86-88; 19. 9-10, 19. See also 16. 101, 137.

40. Francis Jeffrey, *Contributions to the Edinburgh Review* (New York, 1869), pp. 35, 38-39, 458.

41. Wellek, pp. 114-115.

42. Cf. "Essay Third," "On the Principles of Genial Criticism" (Shawcross, ed., *Biographia Literaria,* II, 239-243).

43. 19. 9, 11.

44. 5. 154. Cf. 5. 156.

45. 19. 10-12; 20. 305. See also 5. 154-155, 276.

46. "Dedication to Shakespear Illustrated," *The Works of Samuel Johnson* (London, 1788), XIV, 477-478.

47. 11. 59. See also 5. 154-155, 8. 82, 12. 156 n.; 20. 232; Patterson, p. 1005.

48. "Preface to the First Edition of Poems (1853)," *The Complete Prose Works of Matthew Arnold,* I, 3-6. Cf. Coleridge, *Biographia Literaria,* chap. XIV: "The reader should be carried forward, not merely

or chiefly by the mechanical impulse of curiosity, or by a restless desire to arrive at the final solution; but by the pleasurable activity of mind excited by the attractions of the journey itself."

49. 19. 11-12, 20; 5. 156. See also 11. 92; 16. 41-43, 54.

50. 11. 90.

51. 20. 302, 304. See also 8. 317-321.

52. Quoted 20. 304.

53. 16. 253; 12. 320.

54. This count assumes that "The Banks of the Wye" (5. 156) is "Tintern Abbey," which Hazlitt elsewhere praises under its usual title. Hazlitt also mentions, as one of his favorites, a poem not known to be by Wordsworth, "Lines on a Picture by Claude Lorraine." Martha Hale Shackford conjectures that this title is "probably a mistake for Southey's 'On a Landscape by Gaspar Poussin' " (1797) (*Wordsworth's Interest in Painters and Pictures,* Wellesley, Mass., 1945, p. 51). Hazlitt includes these "Lines," along with "Laodamia" (1815), among Wordsworth's "later philosophic productions" (11. 90). I have also assumed, with Howe, that "The Complaint" (5. 156) is "The Complaint of a Forsaken Indian Woman" (also admired 17. 117) and not "A Complaint" ("There is a change").

55. 5. 156.

56. 7. 144; 17. 25; 4. 250-251.

57. 4. 45 n.; 5. 233 n., 348; 7. 96 n., 133; 9. 39; 19. 108, 204.

58. Talfourd, *Memoirs of Charles Lamb,* p. 189; Southey's letter dated 13 March 1817, quoted in Howe, *Life,* p. 201. See also C. C. Southey, ed., *The Life and Correspondence of Robert Southey* (London, 1850), IV, 239-240, 243-244, 247-248, 295-296; Catherine M. Maclean, *Born Under Saturn* (New York, 1944), pp. 326 ff.

59. *Henry Crabb Robinson on Books and their Writers,* I, 169-170. See also Baker, p. 345; Howe, *Life,* pp. 72-74, 170-171; Maclean, pp. 360, 360 n.

60. *The Times Literary Supplement,* No. 2082 (27 Dec. 1941), p. 660.

61. Wordsworth, *Letters,* II, 746-749, 781-782.

62. 5. 163-164; 11. 90, 94.

63. 17. 117; 5. 156. See also 4. 92; 19. 24. In addition, Hazlitt quotes —with approval of the sentiments therein—lines from "The Borderers," "Expostulation and Reply," "The Fountain," "My heart leaps up," "Personal Talk," and "The world is too much with us."

64. Cf. John Jones, *The Egotistical Sublime* (London, 1954), pp. 60-64.

65. Charles Williams, *The English Poetic Mind* (Oxford, 1932), p. 160.

66. F. W. Bateson, *Wordsworth: A Re-interpretation,* 2d ed. (London, 1956), pp. 142-143.

67. See *ibid.,* p. 140.

68. 1. 185.

VII

1. See Baker, p. 193 n.

2. 6. 91.

3. 4. 226.

4. See also 7. 304-306, 310; 12. 5-17.

5. 8. 242-243. Hazlitt uses italics to designate his own occasional use of "*cant* or *slang* phrases" (8. 243-244). Regarding coinages, Hazlitt accepts the responsibility only for *impersonal* "applied to feelings" and even that in an "abstruse metaphysical discussion" (8. 244).

6. 8. 242-244. See also 12. 250.

7. 8. 6, 79; 12. 61, 125. See S. C. Wilcox, *Hazlitt in the Workshop: The Manuscript of "The Fight"* (Baltimore, 1943), which shows that Hazlitt revised "The Fight" considerably. See also Charles and Mary Cowden Clarke, *Recollections of Writers* (New York, n.d.), pp. 60-61; and Bryan Waller Procter, *An Autobiographical Fragment and Biographical Notes* (London, 1877), p. 178.

8. 8. 244-245.

9. 12. 337. See also 5. 103, 8. 82-83, 11. 89; and note 80 (below, p. 196).

10. 7. 312.

11. 12. 10.

12. 7. 303.

13. 7. 303-304. See also 12. 11.

14. 12. 12.

15. *Letter to a Noble Lord,* in *Works,* V, 210-211. Quoted 12. 11-12.

16. 4. 152.

17. 12. 10-11.

18. 12. 10.

19. 12. 10-11. See also 7. 311.

20. 7. 310. Cf. 5. 54. See also 7. 312; 12. 11.

21. 7. 310. Cf. 4. 175.

22. 7. 303; 1. 185.

23. 1. 95-96.

24. 1. [179], 188, 242, 357.

25. See also *Liber Amoris* (1823) (9. 156-159) and *Notes on a Journey Through France and Italy* (1826) (10. 90, 106, 302, *et passim*).

26. See also *Conversations of Northcote* (1830).

27. 8. 47-48; Howe, *Life,* p. 240; S. C. Wilcox, "Hazlitt on Systematic in Contrast to Familiar Composition," *Modern Language Quarterly,* II (1941), 185-186.

28. 16. 133-134.

29. 17. 107.

30. 8. 9.

31. 11. 134, 69-70.

32. 12. 10. See above, pp. 153-154.

33. 11. 69.

34. 11. 68.

35. *Antony and Cleopatra,* IV. iv. 1-14. See above, pp. 74-75.

36. 12. 12.

37. 4. 105. See above, pp. 96-97.

38. 8. 326, 330.

39. 9. 13.

40. See especially the beginning of his letters to the Duke of Grafton

dated 8 July 1769 and 14 Feb. 1770 and to the Duke of Bedford dated
19 Sept. 1769 (C. W. Everett, ed. *The Letters of Junius*, London, 1927,
pp. 68, 100, 148). When he was a young man, Hazlitt numbered Junius,
along with Burke and Rousseau, among his "three favourite writers"
(12. 126, 228).

41. 11. 126. Cf. especially Junius' letter to the Duke of Grafton dated
30 May 1769: "It is not that you do wrong by design, but that you
should never do right by mistake" (*Letters*, p. 57). Even closer to this
is Hazlitt's sentence (also addressed to Gifford): "What seem your wilful blunders are often the felicity of natural parts, and your want of
penetration has all the appearance of unaffected petulance" (9. 15).

42. Hazlitt had been writing "characters" since the *Free Thoughts
on Public Affairs* (1806) and the *Eloquence of the British Senate* (1807),
and perhaps the early character writers had some influence on his curt
style. However, although Hazlitt "like[d] to read a well-penned character" (12. 229) and although he quotes twice from Overbury's character
of a "fair and happy milkmaid" (5. 99, 141), he seems to have read but
little in the genre earlier than Addison and Steele.

43. 9. 165.

44. Nos. 401, 127 (9. 225, 188).

45. "Si nous n'avions point d'orgueil, nous ne nous plaindrions pas
de celui des autres" (No. 34) (*Réflexions, sentences et maximes morales*,
Paris, 1853, p. 19); "La chasteté des femmes est l'amour de leur réputa-
tion et de leur repos" (No. 88) (*La première Rédaxion des maximes*,
Paris, 1927, p. 21).

46. See above, pp. 111-113.

47. Nos. 46, 70 (9. 169-170; 178), *et passim*.

48. 9. 203-204.

49. Logan Pearsall Smith, ed., *A Treasury of English Aphorisms*
(London, 1928), p. 34. The subsequent pages in Smith's book contain
some additional mistakes about Hazlitt.

50. Nos. 11, 27, 30, 44, 50, 131-140, *et al.* (9. 168, 170, 171, 172, 174,
189, *et passim*). In No. 25, as in the *Essay*, Hazlitt explains that "the
secret of our self-love is just the same as that of our liberality and can-
dour" (9. 170).

51. 7. 310.

52. "The grossest and basest sophistry"; "fitted by nature and habit
for the studies and labours of the closet" (7. 228). For further examples
and an interesting analysis of Hazlitt's style, see Zilpha Chandler, *An
Analysis of the Stylistic Techniques of Addison, Johnson, Hazlitt, and
Pater* (University of Iowa Humanistic Studies, Vol. IV, No. 3, 1928),
esp. pp. 63-69.

53. 5. 69. See also 1. 166; 7. 226; 11. 69, 85, 114-116.

54. W. S. Maugham, "After Reading Burke," in *The Vagrant Mood*
(London, 1952), pp. 142-143.

55. 7. 302.

56. 7. 302-303.

57. 7. 99. See also 4. 201-202, where parallel phrases, with internal
variation, lead rhythmically up to the climax of *Othello*.

58. For a more favorable evaluation of *Liber Amoris,* see Charles Morgan, "Introduction to the Liber Amoris," in *Liber Amoris and Dramatic Criticisms by William Hazlitt* (London, 1948), pp. 7-28.

59. 7. 297-299, for instance.

60. 6. 327-328. Stewart C. Wilcox notes that "of the forty pieces in *The Round-Table,* six begin with a terse observation; and seven pieces in *Table-Talk* and *The Plain Speaker* start off similarly." Professor Wilcox adds that in Bacon's and Hazlitt's essays the initial aphorisms are more integral with the rest of the essay than in Montaigne or Johnson. ("Hazlitt's Aphorisms," *Modern Language Quarterly,* IX, 1948, 422-423.)

61. 9. 15. I am grateful to Mrs. Juanita H. Williams for pointing out this paragraph in her unpublished paper on "The Style of Hazlitt's Political Writing."

62. See above, p. 81.

63. 88. 321-322.

64. 8. 322-323.

65. 8. 373. Cf. Baker, p. 170 n.

66. 8. 323-326.

67. See above, p. 159. Hazlitt, of course, had lost two children. Another time when Hazlitt writes "I never . . . but once," the allusion is not, as far as I know, autobiographical (1. 283).

68. 8. 326-327. See also Adam Smith, *The Theory of Moral Sentiments,* 2d ed. (London, 1761), pp. 8-10.

69. 8. 327.

70. 8. 328-330.

71. 8. 77-79, 79-83, 83-86, 86-89.

72. 8. 90-101, 255-264.

73. *Memoirs of Charles Lamb,* p. 183. De Quincey's judgment is harsher: see *The Collected Writings of Thomas De Quincey,* V, 236-238.

74. 11. 29. Cf. *Antony and Cleopatra,* IV. 4. 9-11.

75. 11. 41; 17. 77. Cf. *The Canterbury Tales,* I (A), 167.

76. 11. 20. Cf. *The Canterbury Tales,* I (A), 150.

77. 1. 242.

78. For example, "when wind and rain beat dark November down" (18. 361. Cf. *Cymbeline,* III. iii. 37). See Stanley Jones, "An Unidentified Shakespearean Allusion in Hazlitt," *English Studies,* XLV (April 1964), 126-129.

79. 12. 228.

80. See note 9 above. The additional references to links in the associational chain have been supplied by J.-C. Sallé, "Hazlitt the Associationist," *Review of English Studies,* XV, N. S. (1964), 38-51. This excellent article, which I had not read before the first printing of this book, strengthens my interpretation of the passage in 12. 337.

Index